To George
Love Aunt Jamie
July 9th 1992

TEXAS
CHEERLEADERS

The Spirit of America

JOHN HAWKINS

St. Martin's Press

NEW YORK

TEXAS

CHEERLEADERS

To my dad (John Hawkins, Sr., deceased), who cheered all my dreams; to Texas cheerleaders whose contagious positivity inspired this project; and to cheerleaders from sea to shining sea whose devotion to making a difference through spirit leading makes good ole USA a better place in which to live.

Design by Judy Dannecker

Book dummy by Diane Stevenson

Library of Congress Cataloging-in-Publication Data

Hawkins, John, 1953–
    Texas cheerleaders : the spirit of America / John Hawkins.
        p.   cm.
    ISBN 0-312-05972-8
    1. Cheerleading—Texas.   I. Title.
LB3635.H4   1991   90-29127
                                                       CIP

First Edition: September 1991

10 9 8 7 6 5 4 3 2 1

Christy Ficthner's rise to stardom began with this Western-styled outfit that helped crown her Miss USA 1986 and later first runner up in the Miss Universe Pageant. Cheerleading gave her the confidence to stand in front of a crowd. *(courtesy: Guy-Rex)*

CONTENTS

(courtesy: Dallas Cowboys Cheerleaders)

Map of Texas based on U.S. Census, 1890. *(collection of Jim Fitzgerald)*

ACKNOWLEDGMENTS

A project such as *Texas Cheerleaders* requires the dedication and vision of a cooperative group. I was indeed fortunate to work with some of the finest people in the country whose spirit touched my life in ways they will probably never fully comprehend.

Some deserve special thanks.

Jan Miller, my faithful agent, cornered me when I was a society columnist for *The Dallas Morning News* and shared her vision for our working relationship. Her unwavering support and compassionate friendship makes this, our first project together, very special. Thanks also to her ambitious and brilliant staff at Dupree-Miller: Katy Hazelwood, Sandra Burrowes, Brad Telford, and Susan May.

Jim Fitzgerald, my editor at St. Martin's Press, worked with me to create a concept that evokes pride for all of those involved. Though I would love to take credit for originating the idea for this book, those kudos rest with Jim. His patience and guidance through the intricacies of project development and manuscript fine-tuning will never be forgotten. He was a gem with whom to work.

Many thanks go out to the incredibly capable St. Martin's team. The list includes Alex Kuczynski, Jim Fitzgerald's assistant who was always there when I needed her and who came up with some great marketing ideas; Judy Dannecker, Jeff Tompkins, and Andy Carpenter, the art directors who re-created the excitement of cheerleading visually and designed a knockout cover. Their love of the creative process really

The competitive spirit embodied in the Texas cheerleader enabled former Plainview High School cheerleader Leah Kay Lyle to reach another sought-after goal among Texas lasses, Miss Texas 1990.

shined in this book. John Murphy, director of publicity whose belief in the project ensured its success and made it all fun along the way.

J. Allen Hansley, who provided nearly a third of the book's photos, was invaluable for the completion of this project. A longtime friend, Allen sacrificed much of his free time tracking the cheerleader trail with me, capturing spirit and energy on film. Never a complaint was moaned. Thanks will never be enough for Dallas photographer J. Allen Hansley who traveled the Texas cheerleader scene with me.

Lawrence "Herkie" Herkimer, the granddaddy of cheerleading and founder of National Cheerleaders Association, was cooperative above and beyond the call of duty not only sharing with me the insights of spiritleading but lending me his smiling staff for every need that arose. While there are so many to thank at NCA, these deserve special recognition: Lance and Carol Wagers, the husband and wife team who head NCA's college and high school programs respectively, helped me understand the big picture; Sharon Dewberry, who was gracious enough to allow me the use of many of their great calendar shots; Amy Lawler, who was always a great friend to work with helping me with even the smallest detail; Barbara King, who introduced me to the world of NCA; Mike Miller whose knowledge of dance/drill teams was invaluable; and the great administrative staff of Della Derrick and Brit Broussard.

Gussie Nell Davis, the founder of the Kilgore Rangerettes, whose unassuming candidness gave the book some punch; Deana Bolton, current director of the Kilgore Rangerettes, who gave me a rare glimpse into the Rangerette world and allowed me to use numerous current and vintage shots for this book. Ruth Flynn, director of Tyler Junior College's Apache Belles, for whom I have tremendous respect—I appreciate her cooperation; Josette Garrett, whose photography staff provided some fantastic drill-team shots.

Cooperation from the Dallas Cowboys Cheerleaders was essential for the completion of this book. Special thanks go to Charlotte Jones, who was more than cooperative in providing me photos; Leslie Haynes, Dallas Cowboys Cheerleaders director, who allowed me inside the Valley Ranch dance studio to watch the squad rehearse and helped me with numerous fact-checking; Kelli McGonagill, former Dallas Cowboys Cheerleader assistant director, who made my life much easier at Valley Ranch; and Judy London, sixth year Dallas Cowboys Cheerleader, who was always willing to answer my silliest questions.

To the numerous spiritleaders who shared their visions, thank you is simply insufficient, but here goes: Carolyn Farb, a new and special friend I have come to adore; Lynn Wyatt, probably the most popular socialite in recent American history; Jan Glenn, whose perkiness has kept her "Good Morning Houston" at the top of the charts for more than thirteen years; Donna Kolberg, varsity cheer coach for Duncanville High School; Brooke Stollenwerck, longtime friend and Dallas socialite; Heloise, the syndicated columnist who always makes me laugh; Liz Carpenter, who allowed me to photograph the University of Texas cheerleaders in her infamous hot tub against her better judgement; Bill Melton, Dallas County Treasurer, whose insights and fabulous photos enriched the project; Judge Barefoot Sanders, who allowed me into his federal court to talk about his former cheer days at University of Texas; Kay Bailey Hutchison; UT cheerleader and newly elected State Treasurer; Leah Kay Lyle, Miss Texas 1990; Bob Hamner, producer of "The Dallas Cowboys Cheerleaders," a made-for-television ratings smash; Tisa Weiss Hibbs, Kim Dawson model; Joel Nash, Zoli Model; Kazie Metzger, Satellite

Dallas Cowboys Cheerleader. *(courtesy: David Woo)*

Broadcast Network, whose Fort Worth mother persisted until I called her daughter; Susan Howard, former "Dallas" series star; Martha and David Tiller; and Pamela Graham, Dallas socialite.

Photographers: Again, special thanks to J. Allen Hansley. Gratitude also extends to National Cheerleaders Association; Dallas Cowboys Cheerleaders; Kilgore College; Tyler Junior College; Fred Pitzke; Fred Maroon; Norman Parkison; *Town & Country* magazine; *The Saturday Evening Post*; Kent Barker; Phelan Edenhack; Guy-Rex; Vivianne Moos; Southern Methodist University; Bill Melton; Pamela Graham; Baylor University; University of Texas at Austin; Debbi Blocker; Brian Smale; Patrick Media Group; Greg Lorfing; and the Scholz Sisters.

To my devoted friends who have given continued love and support throughout the trials and tribulations of my being a writer, thanks is truly heartfelt. The faithful include: Daniel Jones Cooper; Michael Ventriglia, Sharon Fowler; Mary Edwards, Doug Wright; John Nelson; Greg Smith; Jean and Toni Mestriner; Carlos Lopes; Paige Nash; Susan Carter; John Moss; Kay Douglass and my brother David Hawkins.

Last but certainly not least, a special thanks to my mother, Lavina Hawkins. I wish others were as lucky as I, to have such a woman as their mom.

INTRODUCTION

When I set out on the cheerleading trail in preparation
for this project, I was truly unprepared for the revelations
that I was about to encounter. I had never actually been
elected a cheerleader, but I was familiar with the turf, so
to speak.

In high school, I attempted for three years to play
football. The exercise netted me consecutive injuries of a
sprained ankle, a broken shoulder, and a badly damaged
shin bone that became infected and nearly had to be
taken off at the knee. As a result, I concluded that
maybe football wasn't my sport.

Nevertheless, my enthusiasm for the sport and its
periphery prevailed, thus leading me to try out for
cheerleader at the University of Arkansas in Fayetteville
in what seems a lifetime ago in the 1970s. My gymnastic
ability, however, did not equal the charismatic optimism
of my spirit. I miscalculated the spring of the mini-
tramp, which was legal back then, and landed splat on
my back.

Cheerleading was more difficult than I had assumed.

When one mentions the activity known as cheerleading, one is generally met with a panorama of
different reactions. Some sneer that such an activity is
superfluous fluff and is relatively unimportant. They
regard cheerleading as a popularity contest that excludes
many and exalts a perky few. These people have
obviously never followed cheerleaders around for an
entire year, but better yet, they fail to see the essence
and spirit of the whole activity.

Facing page: All-American good looks combined with stamina from cheerleading days in Tyler has continued to make Tisa Weiss Hibbs one of Kim Dawson's most sought-after models. *(courtesy: Tisa Weiss Hibbs)*

Below: For more than fifty years, this over-the-left-shoulder pose and all-white Western-theme outfit have signified the five captains who have earned the right to lead the sixty-five high-kicking Texas gals known worldwide as the Kilgore Rangerettes. *(courtesy: Kilgore College)*

Those that proudly wear school colors, both guys and girls, earn that right and they do so every day. Ever-so-conscious of their position as cheerleaders, all are aware that being elected cheerleaders is much more than inclusion in some sort of elitist society espousing lofty ideals. It is a dedication to a life-style that encourages each individual to achieve the best that each possibly can in all areas of life, and not just on the playing field.

After having talked with hundreds of cheerleaders and drill team members past, present, and possibly future, I was constantly struck with the notion that these kids want to make a difference. That difference is a positive

xiv

attitude toward those around them as well as in the world in which we live. They are cheerleaders whether they are wearing their uniforms or not. Transcending pressed pleats and home football games, their responsibility dictates the way in which they present themselves.

Texans aspire to greatness, positions of authority, and unadulterated fame. The outcome sometimes manifests itself in a form of braggadocio that is simply proud chest-pounding in celebration of either a job well done, or simply of life itself. We here in the Lone Star State feel that there is nothing wrong with that. Therefore, when I praise these Texas cheerleaders for uplifting the human spirit, it is heartfelt.

So all-encompassing has cheerleading become in Texas that many are currently touted as school "spirit leaders." Their elected position requires full dedication eleven months of the year. And it is this spirit that is the essence of this book. I was fully unprepared for the contagiousness of their spirit and how it affected me. The spirit of the Texas cheerleader is more than adolescent energy release, it is the spirit and pride of Texas itself.

This spirit, however, is not confined to the borders of the mysterious region once labeled Tejas territory. This spirit is the freedom to love all that is right with the world and use that positive energy to vault into a life full of promise and the hope of a better tomorrow.

Texas Cheerleaders is not merely a rhapsody in pom pon. It is not merely the spirit of Texas. It belongs to each and every one of us.

It is the spirit of America.

—John Hawkins
Dallas, January 1991

(courtesy: Barker Texas History Center, University of Texas at Austin)

CHAPTER 1
BORN TO
POM PON

(courtesy: National Cheerleaders Association)

University of Texas cheerleaders, like Danny Ruiz pictured here, have always enjoyed B.M.O.C. status, turf usually reserved for the star quarterback. *(courtesy: Fred Pitzke)*

Don't try this at home. Years of practice enable Longhorn cheerleader Stacey Singletary to make this balancing act look easy while chanting "Hook 'em Horn." *(courtesy: Fred Pitzke)*

Some say it's the water. Some say it's in their blood. Others say it's a predestined right needing only to be claimed. Whatever the reason, there is no disputing the fact that most little girls after drawing their first breath in Texas feel, among other things, that they are born to pom pon.

The Texas mind-set. For those unaccustomed to it, let me expound. Texas is a state of mind in which Hollywood's celluloid fantasies materialize into everyday realities through hard work, a little imagination, and the right blush. Proper packaging is a worthwhile reality unto itself. Held closely to the Texas heart is the belief that if one works diligently enough, good things and praise will follow.

Being born with a silver pom pon in one's hand, however, does not preclude one from earning one's rightful crown. Hours are clocked in ballet lessons, modeling lessons, private drill and cheer instruction, and beauty consultation. Dallas-based BeautiControl Cosmetics recently teamed up with the National Cheerleaders Association (NCA) to help create the right cheerleader look for the various types of cheer events. After developing a survey and mailing it to target markets, a phenomenal 38 percent response rate was recorded. This is Texas.

"It's a state where excessive grooming is the daily regimen," says Mike Miller, NCA's drill coordinator. "Texas girls possess the basic southern belle mentality, however they just seem to come out of the womb more groomed than those in other states. It's not normal but it is *very* Texan. That's one reason these kids are leading the pack." Their perfection on the field is equaled only by the passion that motivates such unbridled enthusiasm.

When I first began to follow the cheerleader trail, I contacted Betsy Parish of the *Houston Post*. My former society editor competitor, Nancy Smith of the *Dallas*

Dangerous curves, a knockout smile and camera readiness give Alona Wood that quintessential Dallas Cowboys Cheerleaders look. *(courtesy: J. Allen Hansley)*

3

Manhattan is an unlikely place to locate former Fort Worth cheerleader Kazie Metzger, but the president of Satellite Broadcast Network is one of many who quickly champion the virtues of learning to work cohesively as a unit. *(photo: Viviane Moos)*

Times Herald, already had provided some needed ink on the subject and I thought Parish might do the same. Unbeknownst to me, she printed my home phone number (a practice we are not allowed to do in Dallas) along with a nice item "calling all Texas cheerleaders."

When I arrived home from a business weekend in Los Angeles, my answering machine was jammed with sixty-three messages (before the tape finally ran out, thank God) from cheerleaders in the Houston area who had a story for my ears only. At first I thought I had gotten stuck in a 1-976-WECHEER type of practical joke. Then I just listened. In the next several weeks, I listened to hundreds of current and past cheerleaders rave about the excitement they shared leading school spirit.

What I learned is that cheerleading is a phenomenon that changed their lives. It's never a simple case of pom pons on the brain, as their critics may charge. It's not a vehicle for those desperately seeking popularity. It is an illusive spirituality that transcends the physicality of the gym floor. Cheerleaders are converts to a more positive life-style. Just talking with them encouraged me to reach farther for my own true potential. I began to catch their spirit.

"Virtually none of my New York friends would have ever dreamed I was a junior high school cheerleader in Fort Worth," laughs Kazie Metzger, president of the Manhattan-based Satellite Broadcast Network. As founder of the upstart network she is not only a Harvard grad but a combination power broker and enthusiasm builder. Ironically, Metzger graduated from San Antonio's Ray High School alongside classmate Farrah Fawcett, the quintessential Texas cheerleader stereotype. Surprisingly, Fawcett opted for mousse instead of school colors.

"They [my friends] thought it was kind of a fun thing

It takes more than pretty faces to win a national cheerleading title. Tumbling into top honors is Duncanville High School's varsity cheer squad, who have performed together since they were in the seventh grade. *(courtesy: J. Allen Hansley)*

North Garland High School's coed squad flexes perky muscles to bring the house down and a first-place trophy home during 1990 National Cheerleaders Association Finals in Dallas. *(courtesy: J. Allen Hansley)*

to have in my background but really consider it irrelevant now," Metzger relates. Funny thing, though, everyone always asks her what it was like to be a cheerleader. Discreetly, of course.

For many Lone Star lasses, aspirations to wear school colors are directly proportional to their desire to achieve what Texans refer to as the P word: popularity. We enshrine those lucky enough to lead team spirit in a sort of popular person's hall of fame.

"When I was a cheerleader, it was more of a popularity contest than it is today with all the gymnastics," says international socialite Lynn Wyatt. Nondisclosure of the years she was elected by the 14,000 students at Houston's San Jacinto High School was of course a pre-agreed-on condition for her interview. Waving her service personnel away, Wyatt graciously opted to pour high tea herself. Then, resting back on the mink throws on her library sofa, she reminisced: "In a way it was more flattering for me to be elected by a student body vote because it was more myself. It was *me*, not my physical prowess, that got me the votes. It's more of a compliment when you're elected by your peers for your character rather than your gymnastic abilities."

Recognized around the world as one of the truly beautiful benefactors, Lynn has appeared on the covers of *Town & Country*, *Ultra*, and *W*. Mentioned seventeen times in *The Andy Warhol Diaries*, she was the only major celebrity consistently adored and left unscathed. Her name has appeared so often in boldface in Liz Smith's and Suzy's columns that she rarely notices anymore. Somehow I simply cannot imagine this vision of social perfection screaming V-I-C-T-O-R-Y at a pep rally. But then again, I can.

Popularity is something Lynn Wyatt has never been denied. However, popularity alone did not prepare her for her first cheer in the September swelter of the Bayou

"I've been cheerleading for Texas charities for the last twenty-five years," proclaims Houston social swell Carolyn Farb. "It's part of our [Texas cheerleader] spirit." *(courtesy: Carolyn Farb)*

Nobody does it better than this toe-touching squad from L.D. Bell High School in Hurst, Texas. Get your slide rule and go figure the chances of a line this straight three feet in the air. *(courtesy: J. Allen Hansley)*

City. "I thought I was going to die by halftime," she laughs. "I found out it was a lot harder than I ever imagined. But it made me feel good about myself. More than anything, cheerleading is a team effort. It's something you do for yourself, yet it's something that you can't do without the aid of those around you."

Across River Oaks Boulevard and two mansions down is Carolina, the estate of Houston social queen Carolyn Farb. As one of Houston's dynamic fund-raising whizzes, she has drummed up more than $12 million for charitable coffers. She learned her enthusiasm from cheering, of course.

"If we are going to talk about Texas cheerleaders," says Farb, "we really have to talk about the spirit of Texas. It's that unbridled passion to be the best that cannot be faked. It's an intangible, kinetic energy that tells us no obstacle is too great if we accept the challenge. People outside Texas don't know what it is. Writers have tried to describe this spirit for years without success. *We* don't even know what it is but we feel it. We know it's there. It's truly an inherent quality that Texans possess that drives us to be the best."

"Hogwash," argues Kilgore Rangerette founder Gussie Nell Davis. "I beg to disagree. Texas girls are no more special than any other girls from around the country. The only difference is that they *want* it more."

"My cheerleaders do not take a backseat to anyone," says Duncanville High School cheer coach Donna Kolberg. "They are not content to simply be the pretty young things on the sidelines. Any of the coaches would love to have these athletes on their teams. They want a piece of their own glory, not just to share the football team's spotlight. They have earned it."

For some, being a cheerleader can be life's single opportunity to bask in group adulation. A Houston junior high school student told me why she was so determined to make the squad: "By the time I reach adulthood, I won't be cute anymore. So I've got to grab it now while I can. There will be plenty of time to be old and boring after I graduate from high school." She maintains, unfair as it may seem, that for some, beauty lasts only a season. Making the most of one's fifteen minutes is important.

The pressure to become a Texas cheerleader exacts a high price for this teenager, stuck in an extracurricular merry-go-round. Contrary to her misguided notion, cheerleading is not life, but rather a life-style. She is painfully cognizant that no matter what happens later in life, she will *always* remember that she was a cheerleader. And she's right.

Those outside the Texas cheerleading realm point out that all of this pressure and excessive grooming is obsessive. We don't deny it. In fact, we're proud that it is admittedly Texan. Despite determined vows from relocating out-of-staters desperately grasping a semblance of controlled objectivity in such matters, the spirit is more contagious than the Asian flu. It is the drive, the attitude of grabbing all the gusto, that perpetuates Texas cheerleader superiority.

Let's stop a minute. Why do we have cheerleaders in the first place? FOOTBALL.

Like everything else in Texas, football is *big*. School districts rarely hear a discouraging word when raising taxes for athletic department expansions. It is not uncommon for high schools to sport stadiums with more than 20,000 seats and general athletic facilities rivaling those of most colleges around the country. Wealthier districts not only have provided stadium seats (like those in Texas Stadium) for the home boosters but also have installed AstroTurf. Highland Park in Dallas was the first high school in the country to do so—so long ago, mind you, that by 1990 new AstroTurf replaced the worn.

Growing up in my hometown of Texarkana, both high

Voted Head Cheerleader by her 14,000 peers at Houston's San Jacinto High, international socialite Lynn Wyatt laughs, "I haven't stopped yelling since." *(photo: Norman Parkinson)*

Strutting Texas stuff is what the Kilgore Rangerettes do best. Founder Gussie Nell Davis says pride in a straight line is all the reward they get. *(courtesy: Kilgore College)*

schools had stadium capacities of more than 12,000. Given that the town's population was only 50,000, it easily could be said that on any particular Friday evening in the fall, half of the citizenry was perched in the stands watching the team, or the cheerleaders, the drill team, the band majorettes, or the pom pon squad.

Once a cheerleader, always a cheerleader. The fact is that in the Lone Star State, cheerleaders both past and present often are asked to speak at civic, church, or religious meetings, like their star football buddies. This is called "sharing one's testimony," which is the Southern Baptist way of publicly thanking God for the opportunity to beat the hell out of the opposing team.

In Texas, cheerleading is still the only legitimate excuse to miss Sunday school, because of the fact that the cheerleader was often too pooped to pray. By Sunday morning even God rested after a hectic week. Therefore it should come as no surprise when Mom intercepts Sunday afternoon phone calls to her cheerleader daughter, saying, "I'm sorry Katie can't speak with you now, she's resting her voice."

My quest to find out why so many teenage girls wanted to be Texas cheerleaders was not met with the standard anticipated gushes. Without breaking stride, most of the cheerleaders responded to my question "Why do you want to be a cheerleader?" with another question, amid puzzled pouts: "Why would one *not* want to be a cheerleader?"

They take the responsibility of their position extremely seriously. Texas schools in the 1980s experienced the same strife and turmoil that affected the rest of the country. In an era in which drug abuse, violence, and disintegration of the family are commonplace American maladies, cheerleaders not only lead team cheers but have evolved into respected collective spirit leaders for the school, the community, and the everyday housewife.

Transcending perky smiles and pressed pleats, cheerleaders help set the tone for their schools and for their generation. They are fully aware of this. For them, the joy is in the service of giving, a determination to be the best they can be. It's an attitude that is retained and matures long after a cheerleader has wrapped mothballs around her uniform and hung it in the closet.

There are numerous reasons why a Texan works so diligently to make the cheerleading squad. Of course, that popularity is one reason goes without saying. For most, it is the chance to combine beauty, brains, and brawn, a triad Texans love. Some are natural-born showboats. But there is also the desire to exude positive attributes as a good role model, to develop one's leadership capabilities, to make the world a better place in which to live.

Evangelists and Texas cheerleaders possess similar charismatic fervor and zeal. They both preach that we can make a difference, that we are not relegated to accepting the mistakes of the past as problems for the future. Embracing a higher calling or a greater destiny through the power of positivity is an affirmation that unleashes true spirituality, both on and off the field. It is the power of choice within each of us to exalt all that is right with the world instead of wallowing in that which is not.

Step by step, cheer by cheer, a difference is made. The congregation is growing for those who have seen the light. Their brilliance beckons others to join. The fact that so many are straining muscles vying for the opportunity to wear school colors gives me hope for the future.

Grabbing one's pom pons and inspiring a crowd to cheer is an exercise in exalting the human spirit. In that sense, I wish we were all born to pom pon.

This 1950s Hollywood performance paired two American originals, the Kilgore Rangerettes and John Wayne. No one loved them more than "the Duke," at least according to the girls that were there. *(courtesy: Kilgore College)*

11

CHAPTER 2

YOU'VE COME A LONG WAY, BETTY SUE

The History of It All

(courtesy: Southern Methodist University)

(courtesy: Southern Methodist University)

(photo: Fred Maroon)

These UT cheerleaders have plenty of reason to smile. The Longhorns dominated national football rankings in the early and mid-1960s. Far right is head cheerleader David Northington who now heads Lady Bird Johnson's National Wildflower Research Center in Austin. *(courtesy: Bill Melton)*

Betty Sue the cheerleader wasn't always the darling of the gridiron. Not because she wasn't always darling but because she did not have a football game to preside her darlingness over. Trust me, in Texas, Betty Sue was waiting ever so impatiently for her karma to fall in line, thus granting her the power of the pom pon.

Historically speaking, cheerleaders are a relatively new phenomenon. Directly tied to the sport of football, both have existed only since the late 1880s. Surprisingly, both are American innovations.

There are those Texans who delight in spinning campfire yarns of cheerleaders' humble European beginnings. We here in Texas seem overly concerned with our ancestral backgrounds, all of which seem to spring from royal fountains, mind you. Rarely does one find a native Texan who admits to a plundering, pilfering, peasant heritage. Read my lips: ain't no horse thieves on our side of the family.

One Aesop-worthy tale purports that in the Middle Ages, miserable maidens would follow tawdry townsmen into battle to encourage defeat of the barbaric intruders. Their cheers or encouragements, vocalized from a safe distance, of course, supposedly inspired the home villagers to victory over the visiting barbarians.

Good story, but . . .

Okay, so we weren't exactly off to a royal start and our ancestors weren't actually dying for letter sweaters, but Europeans' lack of fascination with their own brand of football and cheerleaders has little to do with the fact that they did not think of it first. Both are foreign concepts to them. Though football and cheerleading are gaining ground in various parts of the world, primarily Japan, the reality is that many simply view football and cheerleading as solely American.

One simply cannot fathom a pom line at a soccer game.

"Hook 'em Horns, y'all." *(courtesy: Barker Texas History Center, University of Texas at Austin)*

Lawrence Herkimer's mother used to tell him that just once she would like to see a picture of him with his feet on the ground. The sixty-ish Herkie performs his namesake jump on the Southern Methodist University campus a few years ago. Sorry Mom. *(courtesy: National Cheerleaders Association)*

However, do not assume that a lack of enthusiasm in creating their own cheerleaders is tantamount to their lack of interest in *ours*. Our grass is greener inside the Lone Star borders. One is just as apt to find a Dallas Cowboys Cheerleaders calendar in London as in El Paso. The NCA conducts wildly successful summer cheerleader camps in Western Europe and Japan for both Americans abroad as well as local perky teenage pom pon converts. Parade organizers in Europe love to include American cheerleader groups, but their preference is always Texan. NCA spirit groups, Dallas Cowboys Cheerleaders, Kilgore Rangerettes, Apache Belles, and high school and junior high school cheer squads are favorite parade attention-getters, and the organizers know it.

Back to the early history of cheerleading. The first recorded organized yell at a football game (actually a derivation of rugby) dates back to the 1880s at Princeton University: RAY, RAY, RAY! TIGER, TIGER, TIGER! SIS, SIS, SIS! BOOM, BOOM, BOOM! Aaaaaaah! PRINCETON! PRINCETON! PRINCETON! done in locomotion style. In 1884, Princeton graduate Thomas Peebles took that yell as well as the sport of football to the University of Minnesota. There, Johnny Campbell made history with a documented story in the November 12, 1898, edition of a Minnesota student publication called *Ariel*. Campbell orchestrated the election of six men to lead yells on the field. "These men should see to it that everyone leaves the park today breathless and voiceless—it ought to be a revelation to the people of Minnesota in regard to University enthusiasm," he wrote.

Betty Sue simply would have to wait her turn. The likes of Fred, Stan, and Eddie were the only yell leader options at that time.

Texas's love affair with the pigskin began in 1894 with

Less than a year old when this Dallas Cowboys Cheerleaders outfit was unveiled rookie Carrie Blanke worries about the 100 degree heat on the AstroTurf instead of taking heat for what were once considered revealing threads. *(courtesy: J. Allen Hansley)*

17

The 1959–60 University of Texas cheerleaders were the last to wear the old orange "Texas" outfits prior to the introduction of the current signature fringed yokes of burnt orange. *(courtesy: Bill Melton)*

the first University of Texas versus Texas A&M football game, held in Austin. The long-standing rivalry that launched Texans' preoccupation with football was consummated, however, without the benefit of clergy (no prayer) or cheerleaders (no yells). Because the friction between the state's two largest institutions of higher learning was so intense, there arose a need to channel all of that unbridled energy into a form that would produce positive results on the scoreboard, where bragging rights rested until the next year. Hence, the yell leader evolved.

The yell leaders then were always men. Donned in warmish collegiate sweaters stitched with simple, bold insignias, they led the crowd with simple cheers and wide arm motions. Megaphones had yet to be used and public address systems were waiting on Alexander Graham Bell to see the light. As the crowds grew, these

Typical of early Texas yell leading, four men were elected to drum up spirit. *Top*: Bobby Morrison; Flying high are the 1950–60 Yell Leaders from Baylor. *Left to right*: Ed Kenyan, Bobby Schrade, and John Carter. *(courtesy: Baylor University)*

The 1973–74 Baylor University cheerleaders lead the Baylor Bears football team onto the field in typical 1970s hand-in-hand solidarity. *Left to right*: Edith Colvin, Bill Briggs, Anna Beth Shine, Dan Carroll, Debbie Epperson, Robert Woody, Shelley Hudson, and Carroll Fitzgerald. *(courtesy: Baylor University)*

19

yell leaders, particularly at the University of Texas, realized that they were going nowhere fast. A little innovation was needed.

Whether they realized it or not, the University of Texas paved the way for inciting organized crowd responses. Texas A&M did beat the University of Texas to the punch with organized yells in 1905, but it seemed that no one but an Aggie could ascertain what the hell the yells meant. This great mystery still puzzles those outside the College Station tradition.

In 1903, John Lang Sinclair wrote new lyrics to the tune "I've Been Working on the Railroad" for a University of Texas minstrel show as a satire on then–university president Dr. Lambdin Prather. Prather had attended Washington and Lee University when General Robert E. Lee was president, and Lee often had admonished students, "The eyes of the South are upon you." Fond of the quote, Prather incorporated it regularly into campus addresses, substituting the word *Texas* for *the South*.

The song, which received immediate acclaim, was "The Eyes of Texas," which the editors of the University of Texas yearbook *The Cactus* adopted as the university's official alma mater in 1912. Its popularity quickly transcended the university itself, and, like the television series "Dallas," oil derricks, and bottled blondes, it became synonymous with the entire state.

Combining football for macho muscle, an alma mater for school pride, the fight song for inspiration, and a brass-laden band for noise, University of Texas yell leaders discovered the secret for drumming up spirit.

Most people today associate cheerleaders with pretty, young, fresh-faced females. Prior to World War II, however, female college cheerleaders were practically unheard of. The reasons were not truly sexist at heart. University training still was reserved as male territory, so comparatively few women attended college. Today that has certainly changed.

Like many among her generation, Dallas grande dame Harriett Rose enrolled in a fancy New York finishing school, Miss Mason's School for Girls. It reinforced the notion that for women, completing an education was a sign of good breeding instead of good preparation for a career, as was the case for the men. Fondly reminiscing, the seventyish Mrs. Rose says that she and other Texas women formed their own little cheerleader ensemble. The fact that there were no athletic teams to cheer for did not stop them. "We *wanted* to be cheerleaders and we were," she laughs.

By the 1920s, the popularity of cheerleading in Texas high schools, which did allow girls' participation, had already reached such proportions that "every little Texas girl wanted to be one," Mrs. Rose continues.

The women who did attend college in Texas in those days were more likely to be well-bred sorority women more interested in social standing and marrying well than in obtaining sheepskin. (Liz Carpenter is going to kill me for that one!) Not only that, but it was considered unacceptable at the time for women to demonstrate any physical prowess, because it somehow demeaned their femininity.

One must always remember that Texas women are basically southern belles with brass lips.

Things changed when all of the men went off to "the big one," World War II. Women who had been leading yells at the high school level since the 1920s jumped at the prospect now of volunteering for cheerleading vacancies at the larger stadiums. While the men were away fighting for truth, justice, and the American way, some women were busily taking over their school spirit responsibilities. The high school girls who had been cheering with the boys in coed squads or in all-girl

The Baptists were the last to end male sideline dominance. Following a heated student body vote, Yell Leaders went coed in the spring of 1968. *Left to right:* Mike Plunk, Patsy Foster, Gene Cason, Peggy Pate, Warren Guffin, and Mary Matthews. *(courtesy: Baylor University)*

21

University of Texas head cheerleader Bill Melton (1962–63) leads the UT crowd at Memorial Stadium in the traditional "Gimmee a Teeee" yell. Melton, currently Dallas County Treasurer, has been the voice of the SMU Mustangs and the Dallas Cowboys. *(courtesy: Bill Melton)*

Male bonding is nothing new. These 1949 SMU cheerleaders lay down on the job to exhibit unity. Head cheerleader Aaron Spelling is on top. *(courtesy: Southern Methodist University)*

squads found instantaneous acceptance for coed cheerleading squads at the collegiate level.

It was during this era of pennants and raccoon coats that college coeds began to expand their horizons. These new interests gave rise to one of Texas's greatest cheerleading art forms, the precision dance-drill team. Originator Gussie Nell Davis had been hired away from her post as a physical education teacher at Greenville High School in 1939 by the president of Kilgore Junior College, located deep in the East Texas Piney woods town of Kilgore, better known for crude oil than for education.

Gussie Nell's job was to devise an attractive avenue to lure females into Kilgore College enrollment and, at the same time, provide some type of football halftime entertainment that would keep the men in their seats instead of retiring under the bleachers for a nip of high-powered brew. Drawing on her background in the traditional pep club, drum and bugle corps, and military drill team, Gussie Nell added a unique style of Broadway-calibre showmanship to the red, white, and blue Western-clad coeds, creating a truly unique form of American culture, the drill team, which the Houston Contemporary Arts Museum calls "a living art form."

This feisty eighty-five-year-old literally has dedicated her life to the fulfillment of a dream that took form with the Kilgore Rangerettes. Fighting backwater Texas Baptists who originally didn't cotton to her girls dancing on the fifty-yard line, the price she has paid will record her forever as the creator of a truly original American art form.

"Besides," Gussie Nell says with an impish grin, "I've kept the fans in their seats for the last fifty years haven't I?"

Eagerly watching the development of Gussie Nell's new group of East Texas lasses were two Dallas high school friends who happened to vault into the Southern Methodist University cheerleading spotlight in the age of football's All-American Doak Walker: Lawrence Herkimer and Aaron Spelling. Herkimer, or "Herkie," as he is more commonly known to associates, brought tumbling into the mainstream of Texas cheerleading with amicable gymnastic prowess, altering the Lone Star perception of cheerleading forever. More important, in the mid 1940s he originated the Herkie jump, which has become one of the standards for the cheer conscious.

After Southern Methodist University, Spelling left Dallas in his rearview mirror for the West Coast, where he hoped to make his mark as an actor. He later accepted his higher calling as Hollywood's most prolific and profitable television producer of all time. Furthering the careers of megastars like Jaclyn Smith and Farrah Fawcett (neither of whom were cheerleaders, by the way), part of his inspiration and determination stemmed from proudly wearing school colors and spreading the "spirit" of success.

Herkie, on the other hand, bounced around for several years conducting privately sponsored cheerleader camps and spreading the gospel of spirit according to Herkie. Against the advice of everyone but his wife, Dorothy, he decided to pursue his own dream and in 1948 opened the nation's first cheerleading company: the National Cheerleaders Association. No one, not even Aaron Spelling, believed that Herkie's company stood a chance of making a go of it in the business of cheerleading. Nobody but Betty Sue, that is.

Today even Herkie admits surprise that his NCA is now approaching a $50-million-a-year company. It not only administers summer cheerleader camps, it is the leader in sales of cheer fashion gear as well as paraphernalia for every spirited occasion. Most cheerleaders' moms were not even born when he

Clowning around was definitely in vogue for Texas cheerleaders after World War II. Tumbling, gymnastics, and silliness made the SMU cheerleaders the ones to watch in the late 1940s. (courtesy: Southern Methodist University)

23

patented the first pom pon or booster ribbons. *The New York Times* was the first to credit Herkimer with changing the role of cheerleader to one that is now synonymous with leadership, motivation, achievement, and honor.

As the role of cheerleader grew to include other positive aspects of the human condition, so did the aura of popularity it cast on its chosen few. The new allure was only starting to gain steam.

Betty Sue was now beginning to smile—big.

In Texas, as in most parts of the country, cheerleading was relegated to the rumble seat until football overtook baseball as America's sport of choice. Initially it was a club for debutantes, the privileged, the tony ascendees. An attitude of ivy-covered oil derricks. Following World War II, fresh-faced middle-class cheerleaders arrived as the epitome of the bobby socks generation, soon to be crooning over the likes of Elvis and Frank. An innocent era of poodle skirts, malts, and simple GO TEAM GOs.

The 1950s allowed cheerleading to enter mainstream Texas life at every stratum. With some strides toward racial equality coming out of World War II, even the segregated all-black school districts in Texas gained enough financial opportunity to pry open the joys of cheerleading to their students. "Black is beautiful" was the cheerleader in a segregated school, a source of neighborhood pride as well as individual popularity. But one thing changed cheerleading life forever: television.

Texas college football in the 1950s and 1960s was king and the envy of the country. The University of Texas was headed for an undefeated national football championship in 1963. The Dallas Cowboys led their first team onto the Cotton Bowl field in 1960 and already were wallowing in enough success to hastily begin plans for a new domed stadium, which eventually would materialize as Texas Stadium. Gussie Nell had jetted her Rangerettes around the globe several times and halftime at major Texas football games was not complete without some sort of cheerleading show.

When football became highly televised, cameramen soon tired of zooming in on the bruised buns of the star quarterback. Their cinematic shutters began wandering toward the sidelines and the lip-glossed Texas cheerleaders, who were winning over more than just voyeur affection. They started receiving valuable airtime.

Perky, sexy, blond, buxom, leggy, and polished, these were not nouvelle glitteratti queens. They had been practicing a lot. Other states may pride themselves with fresh-faced beauties of their own, and rightfully so, but no one could boast louder than the Texans who held the corner on the market of worthwhile talent and bone structure. During the 1960s, there was a distinct difference. There was no denying that Texas cheerleaders exuded something exceptional. It was their charisma on and off the field that the camera focused on time and time again.

"Our time had arrived . . . we knew it then," says Dallas attorney and State Treasurer Kay Bailey Hutchison, a former University of Texas law student who led Longhorn cheers during the 1963 national championship. "The media treated us like celebrities as much or more so than the football players. They were always interested in sidebars like who was dating who and of course what was it like to be a Texas cheerleader."

Eyeing the enviable spotlight on Texas's college cheerleaders was a group of hardworking Dallas–Fort Worth area high school students who then doubled as Dallas Cowboys Cheerleaders. Riding outside the current wave of their college friends' popularity was difficult enough, but the late 1960s' restless hippies and their antiestablishmentarianism were working their last perky nerve. Apathy has no place in cheerleading or for those

Facing page: Aaron Spelling once held top goal post honors in Texas cheering life as SMU's head cheerleader. Now, the Dallas native reigns as the world's most successful Hollywood television producer. *(courtesy: Southern Methodist University)*

Back flips were UT crowd pleasers in the early 1960s but delegated for men only. Here, Longhorn head cheerleader Bill Melton flips partner Bob Lowe. *(courtesy: Bill Melton)*

25

who need to be cheered. Then Tex Schramm, former manager of the Dallas Cowboys football organization, made a startling discovery: pro football fans rarely wanted to cheer along like the college fans did.

During the height of Vietnam and the all-encompassing general dissatisfaction thereof, Schramm took a risk that the public just might rather be entertained by a lineup of skimpily clad dancers with blue and white pom pons than coerced into rah-rahs by traditional-looking cheerleaders. In 1972, he unveiled seven halter-topped bombshells in white go-go boots, embodying the essence of what we now know as the most famous cheerleaders of all time, the Dallas Cowboys Cheerleaders. Betty Sue was now ecstatic. After all, Phyllis George, a former Denton High School and North Texas State University cheerleader, recently had been crowned Miss America, thus fulfilling every little Texas girl's dream: both popular cheerleader *and* beauty queen. And now this!

The Texas fascination with spunky cheerleaders was ripe for the camera. Light-years ahead of the rest of the country, these bouncing belles increased football ratings and attendance as much or more than the star athletes themselves. Choreographed by Texie Waterman, the Dallas Cowboys cheerleader was the first to bring New York–style jazz dancing to the AstroTurf. The fans loved it.

At a time when Texas college football was grilled by *Texas Monthly Magazine* for slipping in prominence ("only two things are certain, death and Texas"), the Dallas Cowboys Cheerleaders strutted into the hearts of admirers worldwide. The Cowboys were America's team, and Tom Landry's God Squad and the Dallas Cowboys Cheerleaders became the sweethearts of "Monday Night Football."

There they stood, the Dallas Cowboys Cheerleaders,

poised and ready for action at Super Bowl X in Miami. It was 1976, and this was the first Super Bowl in which women participated. The world was watching. So were the cameramen. During a lull in the action and before the squad could break into a routine, Betty Sue incarnated as a Dallas Cowboys cheerleader, threw her hair around, looked straight into a camera lens, and innocently winked at the 75 million viewers. Betty Sue was now a full-fledged superstar.

While Texas cheerleaders were busily regrouping in the 1970s trash disco era, the Dallas Cowboys Cheerleaders were making ratings-smashing made-for-television movies, signing autographs at the White House, and entertaining the troops in energy-draining USO tours in Vietnam during the holidays. So popular was the 1970s female cheerleader that interest among males trying out for cheerleader waned to the point that many high schools simply employed all-girl squads. The cheerleader's popularity had never been greater, but the men felt left out. Until competitions, that is.

For years NCA resisted the temptation to establish cheer competitions, even though its competitors surged ahead with wildly staged competitions, decrying that these antics were unsafe for the cheerleaders as well as difficult to judge. But Herkie, the granddaddy of cheerleading, was not to be outdone. The 1980s belonged to those strong enough to compete head-to-head with other cheerleading squads from around the country. NCA developed its own parameters for cheer competition, which have been adopted by almost every other cheer group in the country. Men quickly flocked back to the sport.

Texas squads walked away with most of the awards from the 1990 NCA National Cheerleader Competition held in Dallas. The *Los Angeles Times* reported in the fall of 1989 that in the Northeast, female cheerleaders

"The case of the yell leaders might be likened to that of the line on a football team. They receive little credit, yet their services are absolutely necessary," acknowledged the 1925 *Cactus*, the University of Texas Yearbook. As was the custom in the 1920s, yell leaders were known only by their last names. *Left to right:* Payne, Penix, Gerhardt, and Robinson. *(courtesy: Barker Texas History Center, University of Texas at Austin)*

27

Dishing attitude is one of the things Betty Sue does best. (courtesy: J. Allen Hansley)

were deserting the sidelines for the playing field, thus hammering the death knell for cheerleading as we knew it. The writer's rationale held that the decline of cheerleading (in the Northeast, mind you) was directly proportional to the ascension of girls' sports. The girls would rather play than sway.

Obviously that writer had never been to Texas. In the fall of 1989, so many kids who really, really wanted to become cheerleaders tried out at Highland Park's McCollough Middle School that the administration allowed all 157 tryouts to lead cheers. The logistics were mind boggling but workable nonetheless. And yes, most of these girls participated in their own athletic events as well as in cheerleading.

The 1980s watched cheerleading develop into such a physically demanding activity that cheering evolved into its own respected sport. Now many of the high school coaches would love to have any of the guys or girls on the cheer squads as players on their particular team. No longer is it enough to be perky, popular, or pretty. Enter the words *strength*, *agility*, *gymnastics*, and *leadership*.

If football is Texas's state religion, then cheerleaders are its evangelists, singing proverbial praises for their teams, their schools, and sometimes the entire state. Evangelists and cheerleaders both must possess extraordinary zeal, charismatic fervor, and an undying devotion to the cause to be successful. Without soul, there is no spirit. Without spirit, there is no magic. For Texans, where there is no magic, why bother? Betty Sue agrees.

Racking up another Division II national title is Trinity Valley Community College from Athens, Texas. Their cheerleaders are heavily recruited by major universities around the country. *(courtesy: J. Allen Hansley)*

The Kilgore Rangettes were the nation's first to effectively incorporate props into the gridiron's half-time show and the only group to glamorize the oil derrick. *(courtesy: Kilgore College)*

(courtesy: Barker Texas History Center, University of Texas at Austin)

CHAPTER 3
THE ROAD TO GLORY

It's the glory. They're good kids and all that, but it's the glory that keeps them going. Once they get a taste of it, they don't want to go without it.

—A CHEERLEADER COACH

(courtesy: Kilgore College)

Voted in 1990 as one of the Ten Most Beautiful
Women in Texas by *Texas Monthly* magazine,
Texarkana's Carrie Blanke is one of a rare few who
made the Dallas Cowboys Cheerleaders the first time
out. *(courtesy: J. Allen Hansley)*

The road to glory, the hallelujah trail, whatever
the designation, there is no mistaking that the Texas
cheerleader determinedly maps out a path for pom pon
privilege.

For one to truly understand Texas cheerleaders,
one must realize the passion they embrace. Their
commitment far exceeds the glorious instantaneous rush
of being chosen. Theirs is a dedication to a life-style,
one that Texas cheerleaders voluntarily sacrifice
long hours and inexhaustible energy to achieve and
subsequently maintain. Theirs is a feeling of wholeness,
a willing immersion that repeatedly vaults them to
the head of the class, not only in popularity but
academically.

"So you want to be one of my cheerleaders, huh?"
says a cheerleading coach with one of the Houston area
junior high schools. Pacing back and forth in front of the
hundred or so mostly young girls seated in the bleachers,
this proud cheerleading coach scans those squinting
under the hot spring sun and wonders how many of them
really want it bad enough. Which ones will work for it,
heart and soul?

"If you want to be a cheerleader, you have to pay.
And sweat is the price for that privilege," she continues
with an intensity Debbie Allen wielded in "Fame."
"You are all winners, I can tell that by looking at you.
But not everyone can wear school colors. Not everyone
can be one of *my* cheerleaders. It takes work, work, and
more work and your stiffest competitor will be your own
body. Those of you who make the cut promptly will be
asked to leave egos outside my door. We work as a unit,
not as a group of prima donnas."

With hair pulled back in ponytails, school T-shirts and
shorts ironed within an inch of their lives, these seventh
graders ready themselves for a five-mile warm-up run.
Even at this age, those who truly want to wear school

"We wouldn't do it if we didn't enjoy it," says Pam McGee, 1978 'Horn head cheerleader. *(courtesy: Barker Texas History Center, University of Texas at Austin)*

33

Have you ever wondered what happens to sideline support when it rains? Ask Baylor yell leaders Anna Beth Shine, Bill Briggs, and Debbie Epperson and they'll tell you they stand by their team. *(courtesy: Baylor University)*

colors must first demonstrate long-windedness and perform one hundred toe touches. Cheering is now an eleven-month sport and not for the weak at heart or slight of muscle. Stamina is required, as are leadership capabilities, good personal appearance, and dedication. It is not enough to be cute.

"Honestly, it takes starting them at an early age. It's rare when you can take a squad that has never performed in front of a large group of people and put them in that competitive situation without them choking somewhat or getting so nervous they are unable to do their best," says Donna Kolberg, cheerleading coach at Duncanville High School. Her varsity squad won its first NCA national championship in 1990 with a group of girls she has coached since they were in the seventh grade.

Great football teams are not built overnight. Neither are good cheerleading squads. Most little girls start dreaming of being a cheerleader when they are barely able to walk. Former cheerleaders are notorious for coaxing their daughters into the system, teaching them the basics at an early age. Sought-after Kim Dawson model Tisa Weiss Hibbs agrees. "As far back as I can remember," she says, "I always wanted to be a cheerleader. Since we were too small for any of the [peewee] leagues in Tyler, we formed our own little group in our backyard. Mother sewed all our outfits and we were off and running. We made up our own cheers and took turns being the head cheerleader."

By the time one enters the first grade, opportunities abound for those interested in cheering or drill teams. The demand for cheerleading instruction has become so overwhelming in Texas that most larger school districts now offer cheerleading as a physical education credit. So many kids were indulging in private cheerleading instruction that school officials felt compelled to answer with an alternative.

The American dream is nowhere more vibrant than in Texas. There is always room for another to slice up a piece of privy pie. In this regard, Texans are not stingy. The more the merrier, the bigger the better, whether it be hair, attitude, or skyscrapers.

Texans worship winners and those in pursuit of their dreams. The business community has always welcomed newcomers with bright ideas. Nowhere else in the country is it so easy to pierce the social bubble or flaunt country club clout. Unlike the rest of the country, Texas operates an open society. Texas cheerleaders believe that another star on the walkway of life could be theirs, if they are persistent.

On the other hand, Texans shed few tears for losers. Furrowed eyebrows frown on those who collapse or whose laziness inhibits the successful completion of their dreams. No one wants to bleed from the lashing that occurs when one willingly submits to adversity. In this socioeconomic structure, it is a shameful fate worse than death.

It begins with seven-year-olds. Though the selection process is not implemented until junior high school, at this early age, everyone who desires cheerleadership can participate. Whether through school-sponsored programs or private peewee all-star groups, they gather by the thousands, seeking cheer uniforms. The sheer numbers have forced NCA, the nation's largest sponsor of summer cheerleading camps, to offer a peewee bracket for seven- to thirteen-year-olds. By the time these kids get into junior high school, the coaches assume that most are well equipped with the basics in simple technique and arm motions, posture, and team work as well as realizing the responsibility of leadership and the pressures of being a school role model.

Wherever there is an athletic contest in Texas, one will find cheerleaders. In various school districts where

Nothing stands in between a cheerleader and her glory, even a cold Texas rain. Baylor yell leader Edith Colvin takes it in stride. (courtesy: Baylor University)

(courtesy: J. Allen Hansley)

Prelude to pom pons. Little lasses like six-year-old Anna Elizabeth Hawkins from Texarkana enroll in dance and gymnastic classes, readying themselves for cheering later in elementary school. *(courtesy: David Hawkins)*

fifth- and sixth-grade boys battle it out in touch football, one will find the omnipresent cheerleaders with their sponsors (sideline moms, usually) gracing the sidelines and yelling their little hearts out. In almost every case, one will find little cheerleaders there with their sponsors to boost morale. Beauty consultants already have attended practice to offer advice on hair and cosmetic analysis. Youthful interest in makeup is nothing new for most Texans. Most beauty advice centers on how the squad will look best as a unit.

Jinger Heath, president of Dallas-based BeautiControl Cosmetics, recently established a high school cheerleader teen board, composed of worthy cheerleaders with high academic standards, to guide others with grooming tips ranging from color analysis to field and television makeup. Paired exclusively with NCA programs and summer camps, Heath hopes to expand her cosmetic appeal and sales to what she terms her most visible market: Texas cheerleaders.

Gone are the days when a simple cheer, a sparkling smile, and pressed pleats guaranteed that popular kids with privileged genes would be chosen by a school vote. The sport has become too sophisticated to trust to the whims of adolescents whose glands are in overdrive. The wrong decision could be disastrous. Though some schools retain the popular vote system, most incorporate the popular vote into a three-part evaluation that helps equalize the selection process.

In late spring, when the majority of high school sports have waned, cheerleader tryouts are just starting. The week-long process begins with a popular student body vote, which counts for 40 percent of the prospective cheerleader's total score. Tumbling across the mat into the center of the floor, each hopeful individual performs a lone cheer before their peers, demonstrating optimum gymnastic ability and enthusiasm. Being a member of last year's squad in no way guarantees a spot for the next year. Adrenaline is pumping. Peers are one's toughest critics.

Over the next few days, each prospective cheerleader will be evaluated again by a panel of judges selected by the cheerleading coach. Each performs as before but is not necessarily restricted to the same routine. Judges primarily are cheerleading coaches from outside the area or NCA instructors with no pertinent ties to any potential squad members. This 40 percent of the total score helps balance the student vote and offset fears that the students will vote only for the prettiest or most popular.

The last 20 percent of the score is broken down into two equal parts: an interview with the cheerleading coach, and their teachers' evaluation of the students' leadership and scholastic abilities. In Texas, thanks to Ross Perot, all cheerleaders fall under the same no pass– no play standards as do athletes. In most cases, though, the coaches require stricter standards for academia, requiring an 80 percent grade average.

One must never assume that early training and grooming dashes the hopes of novices or late bloomers from climbing the cheerleader ladder. It just means that in Texas it's gonna be pretty tough.

Carrie Blanke had only dreamed of being a Dallas Cowboys Cheerleader until she was nineteen years old. While Carrie was attending the University of Texas at Austin, her mother in Texarkana mailed her photo and an application to the Cowboys office for the 1989 tryouts, all without Blanke's knowledge. After nerve-racking dance auditions, Carrie earned a rookie position the first time out, having never touched a pom pon in her life. Granted, the Cowboys do not require gymnastic prowess like the squads in high school and college do, but the fact that she made the nation's best professional cheer squad through innate ability and good dance moves indicates that it can be done by anyone with the desire.

(courtesy: J. Allen Hansley)

Lagging behind cheerleaders and drill teams in popularity, Texas pom pon squads are quickly gaining momentum. (courtesy: J. Allen Hansley)

Facing page: The Apache Belles from Tyler Junior College never perform without the school band or their "friendly Apache" bass drum. The buckskin skirts were notoriously short for the early 1950s. *(courtesy: Tyler Junior College)*

For others, another consideration weighs heavy: beauty pageants versus cheerleading. El Paso pageant wizards Guy and Rex tell girls that they must make a choice at an early age to either follow the beauty pageant trail or the cheerleading trail. Cheerleading develops legs that are overly athletic for the runway, they say. Of the six Miss Texas, USAs, whom they have vaulted into Miss USA, only Christy Ficthner had a high school cheerleading background.

Not so, however, for those engrossed in the Miss Texas Scholarship Pageant (which leads to the Miss America Pageant). Phyllis George Brown is Texas's most famous cheerleader turned Miss America. It is not uncommon for girls to find themselves in competition on the pageant runway as well as on the football sidelines. Miss Texas 1990 Leah Kay Lyle and her first runner-up, Leslie Chambers, cheered against each other in the rival western Texas towns of Plainview and Lubbock, respectively.

"It's simply another form of competition and camaraderie," says Lyle, an adamant supporter of both.

For some, the cheering stops after high school. After a virtual lifetime in the spotlight, it's time to quit while you're ahead. Though one never outgrows the perkiness, it's time to move on.

"Get a life," laughs syndicated columnist Heloise. As a former Alamo Heights High School Spur (a San Antonio drill team), she knows how seriously everyone treats this stuff. "It [the Spurs] was the embodiment of Texas high school at the time. Mothers who had been cheerleaders [like actress and Marshall native Susan Howard] had groomed their daughters since elementary school. The fact is, being a big fish in a little pond is better than being a little fish in a big pond. I know how important it is for people at that age. It was for me. But there is life after cheering. I'm glad I didn't peak at seventeen."

Call them "cheerleaders" and you're cruisin' for a bruisin'. The last bastion of the male-only yell leaders hail from Texas A&M University. *(courtesy: Phelan M. Ebenhack)*

When one thinks of Texas cheerleaders, one usually envisions those in high school. The whole infrastructure is so intense that it boggles the mind. But once one arrives at college, it's truly a different ball game. Somewhere in the 1920s, yelling dipped down into the high school level, partly because college football had become more popular and the effect was rippling down to the high school level. But it is high school that gave us the cheerleader.

Theories are hazy, but most cheerleader historians seem to think that "yelling" was simply unacceptable for young ladies, who now were comprising some of the high school's new coed squads. Others think that it was a verbiage differentiation between collegians and prepsters. Others conclude that once gymnastics was introduced and more synchronization appeared in the routines, it no longer constituted a "yell." It was an organized group leading a "cheer." Today, few yell leaders remain. Baylor University and Texas A&M University are the only campuses continuing this time-honored tradition.

Those keeping to the purest form of the idea hail from Texas A&M University. This highly traditionalized university sports five men as yell leaders, elected in the same manner as other schools would choose a student body president. As the world's largest military university, Texas A&M first admitted coeds to the institution in the late 1960s. Females, however, have never been permitted to yell, although their presence has been welcome during Homecoming Court elections. Surprisingly, campus coeds have yet to challenge this female-excluding tradition.

Texas A&M yell leaders keep it short and simple: no pom pons, no fancy flips or gymnastics, no competition as a squad, no long hair. Simple yells, the most famous being "Farmers Fight," and the school fight song, "Spirit of Aggie Land," dominate crowd participation. Corps

(courtesy: National Cheerleaders Association)

41

members are required to stand throughout every football game and yell leaders cue the crowd with hand signals that indicate forthcoming yells. Although those outside the A&M umbrella of understanding admittedly find all of this quite perplexing, Aggies relish it. The noise at an Aggie football game is deafening.

Then there's Baylor. The Baptists' history of male-dominated yell leaders ended in 1967 after several years of campus-wide voting to change school bylaws, thus permitting women access to school colors. Today's coed yell leaders look like any other group of coed cheerleaders at the university level, with the exception that the name remains the same. As is standard in Texas universities, Baylor chooses its yell leaders through auditions held before a panel of NCA judges or respected cheerleading coaches from outside the state.

Competition for Baylor's yell leaders, song leaders (a spirit group formed to cheer and shake booties à la Laker Girls at basketball games), and cheerleaders (an all-girl squad cheering at women's events) is fierce. It is, after all, the only accepted on-campus avenue for dance movements. Baylor made it official in 1989: dancing is *not* permitted. The Baptists rage on.

Cheerleading develops legs too muscular for the beauty pageant runway, according to Messrs. Guy and Rex of El Paso, who have waltzed six Texas girls into winning the Miss USA crown. Miss USA 1986 Christy Ficthner *(top right)* is the only one to have led cheers. *(courtesy: Guy and Rex)*

Anticipation builds as Duncanville cheer coach Donna Kolberg watches her highly favored squad march onto center court three minutes prior to their winning a varsity national championship in Dallas. *(courtesy: J. Allen Hansley)*

We all rage on. Rage is a fire that can consume or give warmth; it can enlighten a world or reduce it to ashes. For some, channeled rage becomes the catalyst enabling the glory to emanate. No one in their right mind would turn down a chance for glory. Not in Texas, anyway.

As for the different approaches one may run into seeking personal glory in cheerleading, two thoughts consistently occur among those proudly waving pom pons, regardless of age, sex, race, or socioeconomic standing. First, the race is half the thrill. Second, once one achieves the glory, it never departs. In the Bible Belt, the axiom is better stated as "once saved, always saved." Certain achievements are forever. Once attained, it becomes one's responsibility to spread the glory around.

"What lies behind us and what lies before us are small matters compared to what lies within us" (Ralph Waldo Emerson). The road to glory lies within the human heart.

(courtesy: J. Allen Hansley)

Hundreds of NCA cheerleaders from around the nation bow following a group performance spectacular at the 1990 Cotton Bowl Parade.
(courtesy: J. Allen Hansley)

43

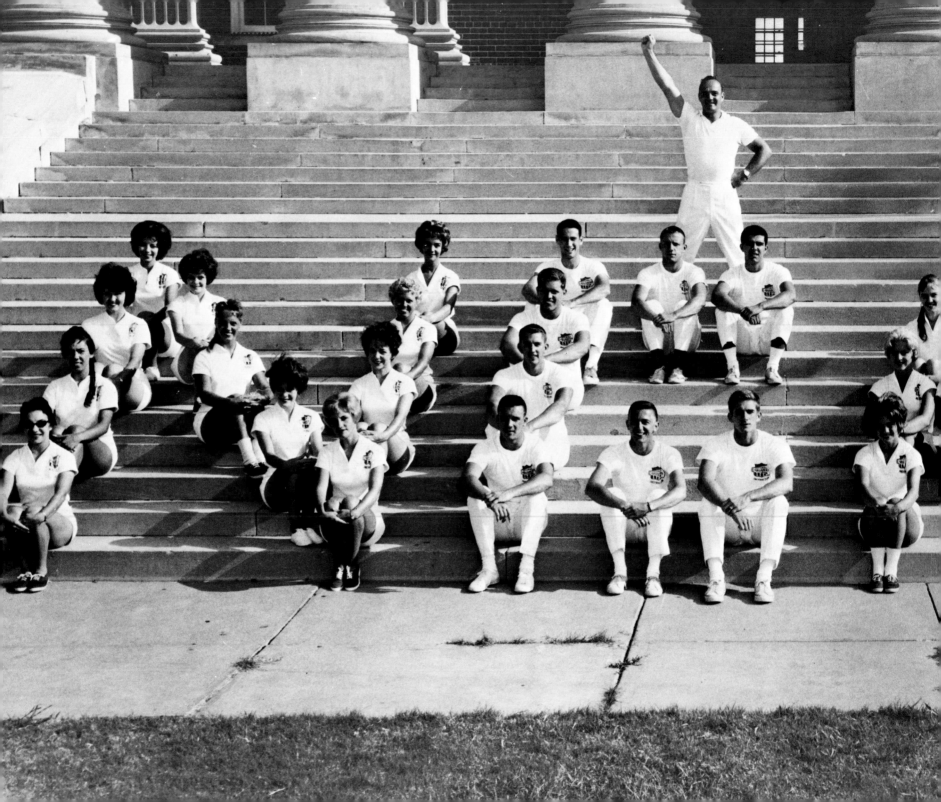

CHAPTER 4

BASIC TRAINING

Cheerleader Camps

(courtesy: National Cheerleaders Association)

(courtesy: National Cheerleaders Association)

This is the only time you'll see Texas girls cry: making the final cut for the Kilgore Rangerettes. *(courtesy: Kilgore College)*

46

Facing page: Doing the "Spirit Dance" at one of NCA's summer cheerleading camps at Southern Methodist University. *(courtesy: J. Allen Hansley)*

"Sea of Babes." If I heard it once, I heard it a thousand times as I watched the NCA camps intently from the bleachers of Southern Methodist University's Moody Coliseum. It's the common colloquialism uttered by high school dudes in reference to the opening ceremonies at one of NCA's weekly summer cheerleading camps.

When you're talking cheerleader camps, it's hard to argue that they get any better than those sponsored by the Dallas-based National Cheerleaders Association. NCA is the largest of all the highly touted camps and is headed by the granddaddy of cheerleading himself, Lawrence Herkimer.

"Looking down onto that basketball floor, man, it's beautiful babes as far as you can see." In a sense, they are right. More than fifteen hundred junior and senior high girls (plus about sixty high school boys) are dressed to shrill in matching school color–coordinated practice ensembles, ready to polish the latest techniques in spirit leading.

In typical Texas fashion, most of these campers are blond. Friends of mine from New York are constantly amazed by the profuse blond numbers in the state, especially in the Dallas area. Revelation for some turns to exasperation for others, but nonetheless, blond remains the Texas state hair color, just as Rolex is the state watch.

As time approaches for the ceremonies to begin, kids start to stand up and wave their arms, screaming—doing what is commonly known as "the wave." As a side note, Kay Bailey Hutchison, a former University of Texas head cheerleader, informs me that the wave actually originated in the 1960s at the University of Texas, although its popularity was eclipsed by the flip card. The fact that television personality Rob Weller claims to have originated the idea on the West Coast raises only a slightly miffed eyebrow in Texas.

High school students are never more attentive than at NCA-sponsored summer cheerleading camps, the most difficult anywhere. *(courtesy: J. Allen Hansley)*

As I stood watching, numerous moms and dads asked me which miniature human on the floor belonged to me. Pausing momentarily to catch my breath from such an assumption, I realized that as a thirtysomething single man (with only three nieces to my credit), I do appear old enough to be the father of one of the darlings wearing matching hair bows and school insignias. There were a lot of parents there.

Breaking my train of thought was a group of more than a hundred football studs from one of the local high schools whose cheerleaders were represented down below. The rough and tough jocks arrived en mass to support their cheerleaders, much like the girls or coed squads rally behind their athletes.

"Get it girls . . . get it," the guys baritoned it out in unison. "Just do it!" Or maybe "South Garland, you're number one." Opening ceremonies are especially meaningful for those who cheer eleven months out of the year with very little recognition compared to their football counterparts. That is changing. The athletes they cheer for have realized the dedication it takes to follow them around and support them at every game. More important, the athletes respect the cheerleaders' physical agility. There are two things that speak to die-hard Texans—physical prowess and bodacious bone structure. The combination of the two is unstoppable.

The man behind me asks me to duck my head so he can get a better shot of the excitement building on the floor. Unbeknownst to me, this fellow, video camera in hand, is filming his daughter and her squad's every move. As it turns out, many of those hoisting hand-held video cams at Moody are not documentary filmmakers, although there are some of those, too. These are dads. In the stands, moms hold court in typical cheerleader booster style while the dads play David Lynch.

Video dads. That's what *Dallas Times Herald* columnist Dick Hitt calls them, himself included. A phenomenon of the late eighties, film footage is the current trend for permanently capturing these precious moments. Seems that so many dads are now sitting in the director's chair that to prevent cam gridlock around the playing area, many high school athletic departments require event passes for those filming pom queens.

Carol Wagers, NCA's high school director, takes the platform as the crowd's roar crescendos to piercing levels. "You are a cheerleader all the time. You represent your school, campus, squad, and you yourself. Never forget that."

One never knows which guest celebrities may materialize at Southern Methodist University, the most popular and difficult of NCA's summer camps. Olympic medalist and former NCA instructor Bart Connors may show up for an autograph session, or even the current Miss America or Miss Texas, Ronald Reagan, or the "Good Morning America" team. There may be a remote telecast for "Today" or a reporter for *The New York Times.* Even Herkie may show up.

As Herkie takes the microphone, a euphoric rush of seeing the godfather of spirit leading produces screams followed by swoons of joy. As Herkie emphasizes all that is right with the world to a new generation of youngsters, the atmosphere turns thick with part old-fashioned camp meeting revivalness reminiscent of early Billy Graham and part Zig Ziglar inspirational motivational messages. The man who elevated cheerleading from a popularity contest into an athletic discipline had something to say. As he speaks, one can hear a pin drop.

"We are gathered here today to learn about spirit leading," he begins. "Spirit leaders are more than merely students involved in extracurricular activities. You will not learn just physical skills. We will also stress

Camps help train squads for the cheerleading nationals. Here, North Garland High School makes a very difficult routine look easy while capturing the national championship in the coed high school division. *(courtesy: J. Allen Hansley)*

49

Yell leader David Duncan rallies spirit for a key play during Baylor's 1983 football season. *(courtesy: Baylor University)*

leadership, sportsmanship, and responsibility. You can make a positive influence in the world today. What you learn in the next four days will carry over to every walk of life and you'll be glad you came. Enthusiasm is contagious. If we could package yours in this hall this afternoon, we could change the world." When he finishes, the hall is filled with screams, yells, and affirmations.

Then an NCA instructor takes the platform and shouts, "Let the games begin." Camp is off and running with NCA instructors, some college age and some in their twenties, performing a gymnastically choreographed routine to the "Spirit Song" (a prerecorded uplifting theme song) followed by the annual Spirit Dance, which all fifteen hundred simultaneously learn immediately afterward.

Following the thrill of learning the Spirit Dance, which

Baylor yell leaders welcome the Bears onto the football field. *(courtesy: Baylor University)*

50

will be repeated numerous times throughout the next several days, the crowd breaks into preassigned groups. My presence, which I had hoped would remain nonintrusive, gathered more attention than I had expected. So much so that when one cheerleader coach from southern Texas discovered my mission as a writer, she wheeled around, giving her all-girl squad a specific cue. The squad broke into its best routine, giving me an up-close and personal look at how *they* could strut *their* stuff.

Momentarily caught off balance, I had no earthly idea what to do now that they had completed their routine and were flashing me their pearly whites. Pausing to collect my thoughts, I broke into a round of hearty applause, congratulating the squad on a routine well done. Quickly making tracks to the next group and feeling a little sheepish, I surmised that all of this was indeed more serious than I had first envisioned.

One must understand that time is not wasted basking in the warmth of one's newly bestowed cheerleading spotlight. No sooner are new cheer squads selected each spring than plans are readied for the year's first adventure: cheerleader camp. Here, as in all of the four hundred NCA summer camps throughout the country, true grit is tested amid the tranquility of fairly deserted college campuses. Cheerleading camp, or boot camp, as many liken the experience, is a great equalizer among new arrivals.

Camp is an intense four-day training ground for cheerleaders, coaches, advisers, and sponsors. It is also a time for squad members to become better acquainted, which eventually enables them to function collectively as a unit.

Those entering camp are housed in university dorms. Because all activities, including meals at school cafeterias, are scheduled on campus, there is little need

Carol Wagers, who's been cheering for more than twenty years, gives daily pep talks to the cheerleaders who attend NCA's summer camp at SMU. *(courtesy: J. Allen Hansley)*

Practice makes perfect. Former Kilgore Rangerette and current Apache Belles Director Ruth Fynn is determined for her girls to be the best. *(courtesy: Tyler Junior College)*

to venture off campus, and most don't. Days for the cheer hearty begin at 7:00 A.M. with stretching and conclude with lights out at 10:30 P.M., usually followed by a pillow fight. Few spare minutes lie in between.

Herkie's staff has orchestrated a program with levels for every group, from the most basic to the highly advanced. The blending of these groups gives incentive to beginners as to what can be accomplished through proper training and sweat. Groups are assured that they will be placed in levels according to their own ability and squad classification. For example, only coed squads learn the latest in partner stunts. Those who need time learning the rudimentaries will feel comfortable knowing that there are classes for everyone. Each student receives equal, intense attention and enthusiasm, regardless of her level of ability.

But camp is not all jumps, pyramids, and partner stunts, although it may appear that way to the casual observer. Students and coaches examine the latest in choreography, the effective use of spotters, how the right use of color and fabric in uniforms accentuates cheerleader moves, how to effectively use makeup techniques and hairstyles, and essential warm-up and cool-down stretches. Updates are presented from Herkie on the status of various states' (and the University Interscholastic League's) lobbying efforts to declare cheerleading a full-fledged sport, which would control activities in ways he feels would adversely affect the activity. Personal leadership also is stressed. They become acquainted with the latest cheers and crowd-control methods. Whew! All of this in four days.

Lest one assume Herkie is getting rich from camps that attract more than 100,000 high schoolers and college-age spirit leaders annually, think again. Camp is one of the most reasonable ways to spend less than two hundred dollars, and that includes meals. While talking with

"Good Morning Houston" host Jan Glenn about her cheerleading days at Texas Tech a brash Marvin Zindler burst into her office professing his strong dislike for today's "cheerleader racket." Zindler is the consumer reporter from Houston's Channel Thirteen who broke the story of Texas's notorious "Chicken Ranch" in La Grange (purportedly patronized by Aggie football players), all of which was later commercialized in the hit Broadway musical *Best Little Whorehouse in Texas.*

Not a Herkie convert, Zindler's complaint was based on the fact that those with lesser economic backgrounds could not afford such pricey uniforms or camps. An embarrassed Jan Glenn strong-armed the mouthing Zindler out the door and we continued.

Serious stretching warms up Dallas Cowboys Cheerleaders before each of their three-hour Monday through Friday rehearsals at Valley Ranch. *(courtesy: J. Allen Hansley)*

I get by with a little lipstick from my friends. Apache Belles hopefuls prepare for the annual tryouts. *(courtesy: Tyler Junior College)*

The fact remains that NCA barely breaks even on cheerleader camps. It keeps the price point as low as possible so that any squad that wants to can attend. Instructors, who often are offered free campus housing, typically earn between $165 and $350 a week, depending on individual levels of expertise and experience. They are all quick to tell you they are not in it for the money. But then neither are the cheerleader coaches, who generally pull in a meager $1,000 extra per year.

NCA even conducts less-expensive, nonresident camps for those who cannot afford the price for the on-campus overnight activities. These predominately urban-area kids arrive on campus every day, attend the same classes, and return home each evening. No one can ever accuse Herkie of gouging.

Herkie generally makes his money through the sales of moderately priced cheerleader supplies. As many people as I contacted regarding the prices for such items, no one —that's correct, not even *one*—expressed the slightest displeasure concerning prices. Most considered the items a bargain for the money.

Because of NCA's success, Dallas can boast itself as the epicenter of the cheerleading world. Regardless of which company or school of thought one may adhere to, NCA and the Southern Methodist University camps are considered by most to be the epicenter for cheerleaders.

NCA was the first cheer organization to put the brakes on unsafe gymnastic practices, such as illegal dismounts, pyramids that were stacked too high, the use of minitramps, free-falling flips, and stunts without appropriate spotters. Observers forget that rules and regulations for the increased level of gymnastics that began to occur in the 1970s were not always clear. Many students suffered hurt knees, sore backs, and broken bones due to the fact that their overzealous natures blinded them to impending dangers. Others attempted stunts above their difficulty range, resulting in potentially life-threatening situations. Organizations such as NCA established safety parameters. To participate in any NCA-sponsored activity or to be aligned with NCA as a cheer association of choice, a squad under the direction of the cheer coach must adhere to NCA's prescribed standards of safety and personal responsibility.

The difference at NCA camps is that NCA has always, first and foremost, been committed to developing student leaders. The NCA philosophy teaches each student not only physical skills but the leadership and moral responsibilities necessary to become an effective school leader and, subsequently, an effective and responsible member of the community.

Closing ceremonies at the NCA are as charged, if not more emotional, than those that opened the camp in what seemed a lifetime ago. Carol Wagers announces the coveted Spirit Stick winners in each category followed by elated screams, congratulatory hugs, and squad cheers. The Spirit Stick means more than just the obvious. It gives those who have worked long and hard an automatic berth in the NCA's post-Christmas National Cheerleader Competition at the Dallas Convention Center and a chance for national ranking or maybe even a national title.

It's now that time when all good campers must load up and head home. Tears cloud visions of newly made friends scribbling addresses amid promises to write and stay in touch. Reverberations in Moody Coliseum and the surrounding hallowed halls slowly cease to echo. But one can still feel an electricity in the air, a positiveness.

Whether they fully understand it or not, what these cheerleaders are left with is more than mere information and a great time; they get to take a piece of Herkie home with them. And that, my friends, is worth all the magic in Texas.

NCA summer instructors are the embodiment of the all-American spirit leader. *(courtesy: National Cheerleaders Association)*

CHAPTER 5

STEERING
CHEERING

Refining the *Way We All Yell*

(courtesy: Tyler Junior College)

(courtesy: Kilgore College)

57

Texans are proudest of the "Herkie" jump. *(courtesy: National Cheerleaders Association)*

Many say it's the Texas mentality. Some claim it's that inherent Texas cheerleader look. Others say it's the fact that Texans revolve around the cheerleading mecca, Dallas. The fact remains that Texans have vaulted cheerleading to a level of sophistication that truly baffles most other Americans. The state's love affair with football, of course, has had a direct bearing on the level of fanaticism in such perky preeminence. The secret, however, lies in the preoccupation with both the personal and professional grooming practiced daily by most Texans.

Though the Constitution guarantees that all men are created equal, not so with yells under the Lone Star flag. Just as the actor memorizes lines, learning yells is merely the first step. But it is the delivery that Texans diligently consider the core of successful cheering. Cheerleaders are in one sense the thespians of the AstroTurf theater performing to thousands in the stands and millions in front of living room televisions. Presentation, packaging, pride. All of these requisites are oh-so Texan.

Experimentation was the original crux of chatter for burgeoning yell poets who simply used the trial and error method in their attempts to solicit crowd response. Upwardly mobile yell masters faced no easy task in scripting yells philosophically compatible with ten-gallon hats and cowboy boots.

Original high school yells seems silly by today's standards:

> *Had a little rooster,*
> *Set him on a fence,*
> *He crowed for the Hornets*
> *'Cause he had good sense.*

58

Or the equally silly

> *Boom boom, b-boom boom,*
> *B-boom boom, b-boom boom,*
> *Send them to the doom doom,*
> *D-doom doom doom.*

East Texas gave us such chicken-fried cheers of yesteryear as:

> *Chewin' tobacco, chewin' tobacco,*
> *Spit on the wall,*
> *Tigers, Tigers,*
> *That's who we are for.*

And a popular chant from then-segregated all-black schools:

> *Bacon, bacon,*
> *Greasy, greasy,*
> *We gonna beat y'all*
> *Easy, easy.*

Uniforms are incomplete without school-colored hair ribbons.
(courtesy: J. Allen Hansley)

No self-respecting Texan would be caught dead without every hair in place. For cheerleaders uniformity and workability are the keys as demonstrated by the pigtails of Houston's Klein High School squad.
(courtesy: J. Allen Hansley)

60

(courtesy: National Cheerleaders Association)

My how things have changed.

For many, cheering has basically come full circle. Simple "Go team gos" that were the standard during the raccoon coat and flapper era are back in vogue. "Two bits, four bits, six bits, a dollar," says Carol Wagers. "We've gone back to simple cheers that the crowd can really follow, ones that the crowd doesn't need a text to see which words come next." Those are your "Go, fight, win," crowd-response cheers. But the phenomenon of the eighties was the performance cheer. Texans literally ate them up.

Performance cheers are those pregame or halftime routines choreographed with the band or recorded music incorporating dance, gymnastics, pyramids, stunts, and school cheers. These flashy four-minute routines are the ones used in the national cheerleader competitions as well as those spotlighted in community-related events. Texans were twistin' 'n' shoutin' long before Los Angeles discovered the Laker Girls.

In Texas, cheerleaders not only evoke crowd response at athletic functions and school-sponsored events, they also perform at pep rallies, mall openings, fashion shows, beauty pageants, hospitals, and charity fund-raisers. Rarely is there a time when the reigning Miss America is in the state that several of the area's best cheer squads don't perform. Judging from the size of the crowds, the only one who may draw a larger crowd is Elizabeth Taylor. Even when Liz arrived at Dallas and Houston Neiman Marcus stores to promote her new fragrance, Passion, she donned her purple Gucci cowboy hat and asked the 8,000 well-wishers, "But where are the cheerleaders?"

The Texas cheerleader look is no accident. Many cheerleader coaches have followed the lead of the Kilgore Rangerettes. For a more uniform look on the field, founder Gussie Nell Davis always required her legendary

They may look like average teenagers now, but in a few minutes, they will transform into Texas cheerleaders and mesmerize a crowd with boundless enthusiasm. *(courtesy: J. Allen Hansley)*

61

Crowds go wild in the stands when cheerleaders break into tightly choreographed group boogie breakdowns. Duncanville's varsity cheerleaders are some of the country's best. *(courtesy: J. Allen Hansley)*

high-kicking drill team to apply a heavy coat of the same blue eye shadow and bright red lipstick. Regardless of skin tone, performance routines demand theatrical-type makeup. The more uniform the look of the group, the better.

Hairstyles are no longer left to individual discretion or fashion whims. Hair is now considered an extension of the uniform itself. Different lengths and styles draw unnecessary attention to one's hair when flipping and flying through the air. "You don't want the crowd to look at your squad and think what pretty hair one of the girls has," says a San Antonio coach. "You want them to see their faces, not their hair."

Houston's Klein High School opts for their signature braided pigtails. Cypress Creek High School likes ponytails. Many even hot roll their hair moments before a performance, pulling their hair back into what appears to be a pom pon on the back of the head. The result is the same: uniformity. Make hair work with the routine, not conflict with it.

Gone are the days when a cheerleader's mother sewed up two uniforms for her daughter: a cotton one for the September sizzle and a wool one for November nippiness. Most cheerleaders today purchase or special order the latest in spirit-leading fashions from Dallas-based Cheerleader Supply, whose annual mailings number more than 1,250,000. With outfits for every possible occasion in their 160-page catalog, one is never at a loss for the right uniform. Staff designers can thrill the cheer coach with perfectly designed togs for the squad, creating a signature look.

Performance colors emphasize arm movements, therefore white or brighter school colors should be highlighted along the chest and extending the length of the arms. Sleeveless tops indicate that the squad's arm motions are not in sync, and gloves are definitely for the

Texas girls love to perform the high kick as much as Texans love to watch. The Apache Belles strutt stuff at a Cotton Bowl parade crowd. *(courtesy: J. Allen Hansley)*

63

Tuck. *(courtesy: National Cheerleaders Association)*

Spread Eagle. *(courtesy: National Cheerleaders Association)*

64

Standard Jumps for the Texas Cheerleader

pom pon squad, never for cheerleaders. Though most of this information is obtained through locker room gossip among the coaches (why should they share tricks of the trade), the on-staff designers at Cheerleader Supply are savvy to the latest in drop-dead threads and would never lead their clients astray.

There are isolated problems with cheer outfits, however. Arlington High School students recently were saddled by the school board's new dress code decree. Though no one thought about it at the time, the cheerleading skirts were too short to fall under the board's minimum above-the-knee skirt length. Coach Stephanie Garner relates: "The girls have to bring their cheer uniforms to school and change into them immediately before the pep rally and then out of them again before returning to class. We would change the length, but the skirts just don't work that long."

Choreography is no doubt the toughest facet facing the high school cheerleading coach of today. One must combine an effective mix of music selection, contents of the routine, the creative process, and the subsequent physical perfection into a fast-paced live music-video-style number that showcases the squad members' talents without allowing the difficulties to outstrip their abilities. It is not an easy task.

"Pick a focal point. Put that one girl up front and center who can really sell the routine. One who can dish attitude and make believers out of those in the back row," says Duncanville High School coach Donna Kolberg. "You want to lead spectator eyes where you want them to go and not drift aimlessly around the group." That's part of the magic in a high school routine. Those who are better dancers should be on the first row, those who are better tumblers should be maneuvered up front during that portion of the routine. Everyone shines for an instant. Everyone contributes what they do best. Everyone gets to share in the glory.

"In high school, cheerleading is more of an entertainment thing," says Lance Wagers. "A lot of the students know the words and some of the dance moves and will participate right there in the stands. All those rhythmic things—stomp clap chants and boogie moves—work well in high school because the crowd as a whole is more responsive. But it doesn't apply in college. If college squads are doing that, it's because they don't know any better."

People remember high school chants, too. Sixtysomething Betty Ewing, a popular columnist for the *Houston Chronicle*, bolted over to me at a swanky Houston soiree and fell to one knee in her floor-length red bugle-beaded gown, yelling, "L-E-O-N-A-R-D. Leonard. Leonard. Leonard," complete with arm motions. With a raspy guffaw, she said, "That's how we used to do it at my own Leonard [Texas] High School." In most other cities, such an action would have been considered, well, inappropriate. But in Houston, guests laughed and applauded. To say that cheerleaders are popular in Texas is an understatement.

Colleges draw heavily on experienced high school cheerleaders to fill their ranks. The University of Texas initiated a system of two cheer squads because the demands on the squad had escalated to such a degree that coach Loyce Bates feared that the cheerleaders' studies might suffer. The squad cheering for the football season is more indicative of what one visualizes as a traditional University of Texas cheerleader: partner stunts and a lot of "Hook 'em horns." The larger basketball squad, however, is a fast-paced coed dance troupe that not only leads yells but builds crowd enthusiasm with high-energy, pyramid-stacking boogie breakdowns. Colleges now assemble various groups

Double Hook. *(courtesy: National Cheerleaders Association)*

Pike. *(courtesy: National Cheerleaders Association)*

Toe Touch. *(courtesy: National Cheerleaders Association)*

Side Hurdler. *(courtesy: National Cheerleaders Association)*

promoting school spirit in ways their forefathers never dreamed. Cheerleaders. Pom pon squads. Dance teams. Song leaders. The designations are unimportant. The bottom line is that more students today are actively involved in leading school spirit than ever before.

Trinity Valley Community College in the small East Texas town of Athens was the nation's first to offer full cheerleader scholarships to its twenty-member squad. In 1984, Trinity Valley was the first and only junior college to compete in NCA's national competition, placing in the top ten every year, with back-to-back national Division II championships in 1989 and 1990. According to cheerleading coach Connie Russell, "Scholarships were offered because we wanted the best possible cheerleaders and we wanted public relations ambassadors for the college. They should be rewarded for the work they do just like other athletes."

The best of the old and the new can be identified with traditional yell leaders at Texas A&M University and cheerleaders at the University of Texas. Hand signals originated with the A&M yell leaders to signal fans of forthcoming yells.

> *Hulabaloo! Caneck! Caneck!*
> *Hulabaloo! Caneck! Caneck!*
> *Wah-hee! Wah-hee!*
> *Look at the team!*
> *Look at the team!*
> *Look at the A&M team!*

Or

> *Slowly . . .*
> *Rah! Chaw! Haw! AMC!*
> *Faster*
> *Rah! Chaw! Haw! AMC!*

And

A! A! AMC!
A! A! AMC!
Farmers! Farmers! Farmers!

Those outside the A&M rank and file have no idea what such yells of past and present could possibly mean. Aggie Land is steeped in tradition and it matters not that outsiders have no clue as to whether to be insulted or frightened by such boisterous proclamations. It's team inspiring and pride promoting to athletes and students alike. "So there," they say.

Ironically, it is not A&M's hand signals that came to epitomize Texas cheerleading. In 1955, a half century after A&M began the practice, the "Hook 'em horns" battle cry originated at a University of Texas pep rally. The hand sign, representing a longhorn steer's head, has become so strongly identified with Texas that other cheer squads, including the Baylor Bears, the University of Houston Cougars, and the University of North Texas Eagles, formed their own hand signs representing their mascots' paws, pads, and claws. University of Texas opponents often turn the longhorn hand sign downward or add the middle finger to the original sign, thus creating, how should one say, a negative "Down with UT" sentiment. But one will *never* see other Texas cheerleaders sanctioning such actions.

Texas cheerleaders eat, breathe, and sleep cheerleading in an all-consuming dedication to a philosophy that not only evokes positive crowd response but awakens dormant possibilities within oneself. But why do they push the limits of perky expectations? Why do they polish routines at exasperating levels? Why do they demand perfection from themselves? The answer lies in the words to the University of Texas's alma mater,

Front Hurdler. *(courtesy: National Cheerleaders Association)*

Double Nine. *(courtesy: National Cheerleaders Association)*

67

The Apache Belles strut Texas stuff. *(courtesy: Tyler Junior College)*

NCA razzle dazzle at its best: Cheerleaders perform in the 1989 New York Macy's Thanksgiving Day Parade. *(courtesy: National Cheerleaders Association)*

"The Eyes of Texas," which, by most standards, has become synonymous with all Texans:

> *The eyes of Texas are upon you,*
> *All the live long day.*
> *The eyes of Texas are upon you,*
> *You cannot get away.*
> *Do not think you can escape them,*
> *At night or early in the morn.*
> *The eyes of Texas are upon you,*
> *'Til Gabriel blows his horn.*

We as Texans have placed our cheerleaders atop lofty pedestals, and rightfully so. Once they get there, they don't want to ever risk falling off, because they know everybody is watching.

Various Texas Cheers—Fall 1939:

> *Alamaca Ching Alamaca Chaw*
> *Alamaca Ching Ching*
> *Chaw Chaw Chaw*
> *Boomalaca Boomalaca*
> *Sis Boom Bah*
> *West Junior, West Junior*
> *Rah Rah Rah*
> (Milton Wilson, Waco Junior High Yellow Jackets)

> *We're the pride of Texas,*
> *We'll put you to the test.*
> *You may think you're pretty good*
> *But we know we're the best.*

Second-year Dallas Cowboys Cheerleader Opal Bush flashes he[r] best smile. Such glitzy cameo shots previously doubled as th[e] girls' publicity pics for special events; currently, they ar[e] mementos of a year of hard work. *(courtesy: Dallas Cowboy[s] Cheerleaders[)]*

(courtesy: J. Allen Hansley)

CHAPTER 6

TUMBLE
FOR THE ROSES

Texas' Best Cheerleading Squads

(courtesy: Fred Pitzke)

71

A prayer for the roses: And lead us into the routines that we have so diligently practiced. Amen. *(courtesy: J. Allen Hansley)*

The Baptists prove they have a sense of humor during the NCA/USA Collegiate Nationals. *(courtesy: J. Allen Hansley)*

The right toe of Donna Kolberg's black high-heeled pump nervously taps against the polished concrete floor of the Dallas Convention Center Arena. Dressed in tight blue jeans, a simple white T-shirt, and an oversized denim jacket with enough fringe and beaded doodads to make Bob Mackie's mouth water, the short-haired brunette carefully folds her arms, lowers her eyes ever so slightly, and looks confidently into the fourteen perky faces in front of her. "Girls, this is it."

During the holiday break between Christmas and New Year's Day, while most Texans are either skiing in Colorado or devouring enormous portions of turkey, Kolberg and her varsity cheerleading squad from Duncanville High are battling for first-place honors at the NCA Cheerleader National Championships in Dallas. Though Duncanville's junior varsity squad has captured the national title for the past three consecutive years, the championship title has eluded the varsity. This year they are the favorites. Duncanville, word on the block has it, is the squad to beat.

"There are winners and there are losers. There is no in-between. This is what we've worked for all year: the chance to prove we're the best," Kolberg tells the squad in her last-minute pep talk. "I want you to go out there and *sell it* to the last person in that top row. Show them you've got what it takes to bring home that national championship."

Kolberg glances to her left, noticing a group of cheerleaders huddled tightly together for a last-minute Hail Mary prayer before they hit the mat for their performance. "All the prayer in the world won't help them now if they haven't practiced enough," she muses.

"I don't want them to peak too early," she whispers to me, trying to conceal the jitters. "Sometimes they can peak before they go on and lose it in the middle of the routine. It's my responsibility to funnel all that teenage

Judges inform NCA high school director Carol Wagers as to which cheerleading squads have been selected to perform in the national finals the following day at the Dallas Convention Center. *(courtesy: J. Allen Hansley)*

73

energy into a controlled situation and to make sure that doesn't happen," she says. "So far we've been lucky."

The girls head back into the wings by themselves as Donna strides over to the coaches' station, adjacent to the judges' box. High school routines are precisely clocked between three and three and a half minutes, splitting the time between gymnastics, pyramid building, and organized school cheers, and the high-energy recorded music segment that comprises dance, flips, tumbles, and more pyramids.

As the squad marches out onto the mat, the screaming six thousand cheeraholics in the stands go wild. Everyone knows that this is the squad to watch. Even last year's champions from Henry Clay High School in Louisville, Kentucky, are biting their nails. Many of the Duncanville football players have cut their family holiday short in order to cheer their support group. "Get it, girls. Get it, Duncanville," the guys wail from the stands.

The fate of national cheerleading titles rest in the hands of judges like this one. *(courtesy: J. Allen Hansley)*

University of North Texas cheerleaders perform "the scorpion" for a fourth place finish at the 1990 National Collegiate Finals. *(courtesy: J. Allen Hansley)*

The Duncanville freshmen win the first of three first place trophies for Duncanville High School. *(courtesy: J. Allen Hansley)*

Trinity Valley Community College from Athens, Texas, has the most praised cheerleader program in the country and several national titles including this one. *(courtesy: J. Allen Hansley)*

The best large varsity cheer squad in the USA: Duncanville High School. *(courtesy: J. Allen Hansley)*

Texans tying for Best Cheerleader national honors are John Houston from McCullough High School, Woodlands, Texas, and Julie Mayfield, Central High School, San Angelo, Texas. *(courtesy: J. Allen Hansley)*

South Garland H.S. captures the National High School Coed crown. *(courtesy: J. Allen Hansley)*

This is the moment Donna has waited for. No novice, this thirty-year-old, who made history as the first female head cheerleader at Southern Methodist University, has conducted summer camps for NCA and currently dances on the Dallas Mavericks dance squad. More important, she has coached this group of Duncanville cheerleaders since they were in the seventh grade. And this time, she just feels a national championship.

The crowd's roar pauses. Donna slips her cassette into the tape machine and punches *play*, and the Duncanville varsity squad is off and running. For a frenetic three and a half minutes, their high school spirit has the fans on the edge of their seats. The girls tumble their way into a near-perfect routine. The crowd feels it, the cheerleaders know it, Donna realizes it. The last beat sounds and Donna is jumping up and down as her kids scream, hug, and cry while trying to exit the mat. They've hit their mark, and they all know it.

The anxious smiles of the upcoming cheer squad taking its places on the mat instantly tug at the hearts of the audience. The girls from this small East Texas town realize they've been outclassed, but they refuse to let their nervousness overcome them. They stand tall, hands on their hips, take a deep breath, and give it their all. In show business, no one ever wants to follow animals or children. Here, no one wants to follow Duncanville. It would take a miracle to beat Duncanville; dark horse finishes are rare in pom pon competition. But someone has to do it.

Braggadocio never had it so good. When the finals are tallied, Duncanville not only captures top honors with Donna's varsity squad but also snags first-place honors with junior varsity and the Duncanville freshmen as well as landing a fourth-place finish for Reed Junior High. Never before in NCA competition has a single school

Veteran contenders, Klein High School cheerleaders regularly make the national finals. *(courtesy: J. Allen Hansley)*

Cheerleaders from Grand Prairie High School face the judges. *(courtesy: J. Allen Hansley)*

Lubbock's Monterrey High School cheerleaders take third place national honors back to West Texas with this spirited routine. *(courtesy: J. Allen Hansley)*

taken home three national championships, and all right in Herkie's backyard.

Prior to NCA's national championships, cheerleaders were judged primarily according to how well their football team fared in the rankings. If one had a championship football team, one's cheerleaders were honored laterally as well. If one had a losing season, many times a good cheer squad simply was overlooked. Bragging rights are no longer a lot of hot air; now there are trophies.

To earn a berth in the NCA finals, a cheer squad must attend one of NCA's numerous summer camps and win the coveted Spirit Stick or various other awards presented to worthy squads. Those that do not attend summer camps must place in one of NCA's fall regionals in order to come to Dallas in December. More than four hundred high schools from as far away as Hawaii competed in the first round of the two-day championship finals. The top ten squads in each category compete in sudden death competition the next day. College squads' preliminary and final scores are combined for their totals.

The judges, respected cheerleading experts from around the country, are handpicked by the NCA staff. Each exhibits a long-standing tradition of excellence in the field of cheering and shares the common visions of NCA. Each squad is judged on a possible one hundred–point total in the areas of technical fundamentals, such as leaps, pyramids, body extension, uniformity of style, and degree of difficulty; projection, such as facial expression, showmanship, and confidence; choreography, including creativity and degree of difficulty; and overall execution, including squad timing, spacing, and use of the floor.

Texas cheerleaders relish the opportunity to tumble for the roses and to assert cheerleader superiority. Not merely a test for the state's bragging rights, it is one in which to flex national cheer muscle as well. As much as

Flipped out! Cheerleaders from national finalist Sam
Houston State University throw their partners more
than twenty feet into the air. *(courtesy: J. Allen Hansley)*

The University of Texas Pom Pon Squad high kicks their way to being the best in the Lone Star State. *(courtesy: Fred Pitzke)*

80

Dallas socialite Pamela Graham *(far left)* was one of the initial Dallas Cowboys Cheerleaders coed squad originally named Belles and Beaux. *(courtesy: Pamela Graham)*

the NCA championships helped to separate cheerleading from football, the two remain wedded.

Southern Methodist University recently discovered that life without the pigskin was no laughing matter. Conspicuously absent from the 1990 championship arena were the Southern Methodist University Mustangs cheerleaders. Following the National Collegiate Athletic Association's (NCAA's) death knell sanction slapped on Southern Methodist's football team for recruiting violations, the cheerleaders found themselves with little to cheer about. Two years of no football sapped the spirit away from one of Texas's premier cheer squads.

In the mid-1980s, Southern Methodist's cheerleaders were the envy of the country. To most, they had it all: a nationally ranked football team, a nationally ranked squad, pretty faces, Piagets and pearls, private school privileges, and pedigreed backgrounds. Bumper stickers on Highland Park Mercedes boasted: "SMU Mustangs, the best team money can buy."

There are other sports, of course, but in Texas, taking away one's football team is akin to shaving your dog 'cause it's got the mange. Southern Methodist University football is rebuilding for the 1991 season, and so are the cheerleaders. Certainly, other schools have had periods of difficulty, but never has one had its team dismantled for two years. Texas spirit leading was put to the truest of tests.

"If all you have is embers, you fan them until you're blue in the face. Never let the spirit die," said a former Southern Methodist cheerleader. "Once it's dead, it's just dead. We couldn't let that happen." Southern Methodist's cheerleaders may have momentarily caught a case of the vapors, but it will pass. Look for them to flip out in full flex soon.

The best college squad in Texas comes from none other than Trinity Valley Community College, a

Great dance moves helped earn Richardson's Berkner High School junior varsity cheerleaders a berth in the national competition. *(courtesy: J. Allen Hansley)*

The pride of San Antonio, Tom C. Clark High School cheerleaders, take home first place honors in the small varsity category. *(courtesy: J. Allen Hansley)*

The thrill of victory is cherished in the hearts of those who earn these trophies, which will soon be proudly locked in school display cases. *(courtesy: J. Allen Hansley)*

two-year institution in Athens. The twenty-member squad has won two consecutive national Division II championships, surprising even Division I powerhouse the University of Texas.

Though the University of Texas cheerleaders rank as Texas's most consistent and recognizable squad, Texas A&M yell leaders, albeit boring and somewhat stuffy, are the most effective at enlisting crowd response. Baylor University lines up the best-looking cheer masters and the University of Houston has the largest group of minorities wearing school colors.

The Kilgore College Rangerettes and the Tyler Junior College Apache Belles are the best drill teams in the nation—no contest there. Neither competes in drill competition, though. They leave that to the high school teams.

The best of the best would not be complete without the world-famous Dallas Cowboys Cheerleaders, the most famous cheerleaders of all time. Since the squad's redesign in 1972, these cheerleaders have pom ponned their way around the world several times and into the hearts of people everywhere. They are the world's premier professional athletic support and entertainment troupe, hands down. Name one other professional squad's name and describe their outfit. Competitions for bragging rights are never challenged. Every professional cheer squad has always compared itself to the Dallas Cowboys Cheerleaders at one time or another. But the Cowboys Cheerleaders measure their success only by their former accomplishments.

The race for the roses does not start when new squads are chosen each spring or summer. The race begins when these kids are born. To suit up nationally competitive squads it takes time, determination, and dedication as well as the willingness to sweat. Cheerleaders must work past their personal best, superseding the notion that

A San Angelo's Central High School coed cheer squad takes to the air for an impressive start in the national finals. *(courtesy: J. Allen Hansley)*

striving to be the best one can be is the means to an end.

For Texas cheerleaders, striving to be the best one can be is not enough. That's part of personal growth. They want to be number one. Period. Never underestimate their desire to be the best. It is a desire that not only springs from their hearts and twitches amid the recesses of their minds, it's in their blood, and that alone keeps them coming back time and time again to tumble for the roses.

Dallas Cowboys Cheerleaders directors Kelli McGonagill *(left)* and Leslie Haynes *(right)* critique their squad's performance at Texas Stadium. *(courtesy: Dallas Cowboys Cheerleaders)*

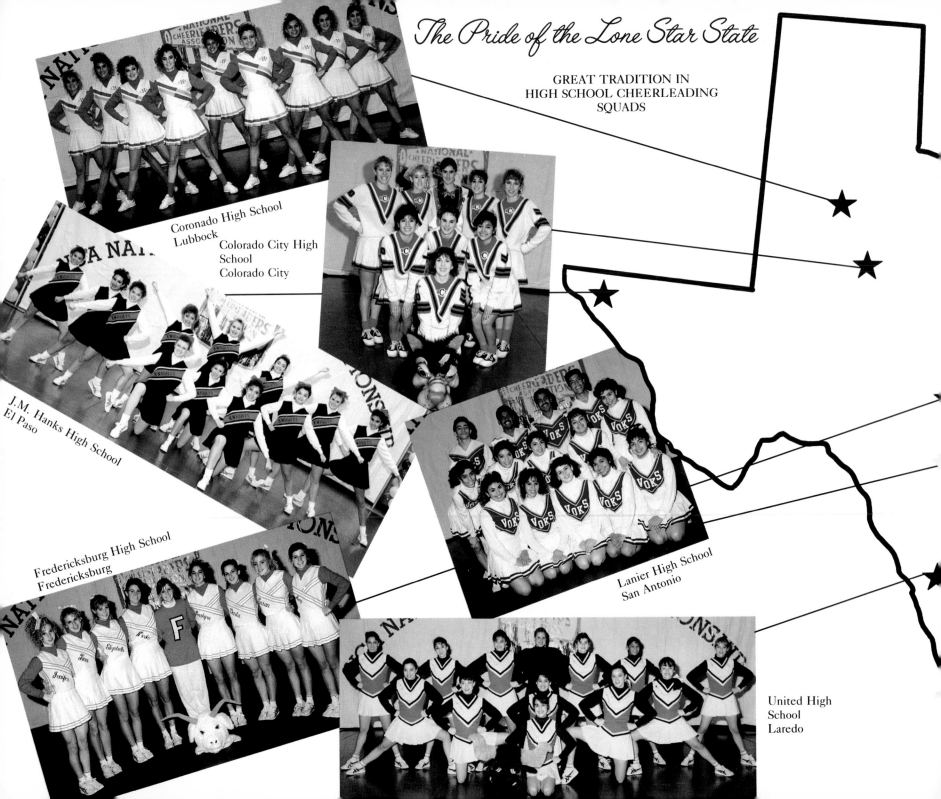

The Pride of the Lone Star State

GREAT TRADITION IN
HIGH SCHOOL CHEERLEADING
SQUADS

Coronado High School
Lubbock

Colorado City High
School
Colorado City

J.M. Hanks High School
El Paso

Fredericksburg High School
Fredericksburg

Lanier High School
San Antonio

United High
School
Laredo

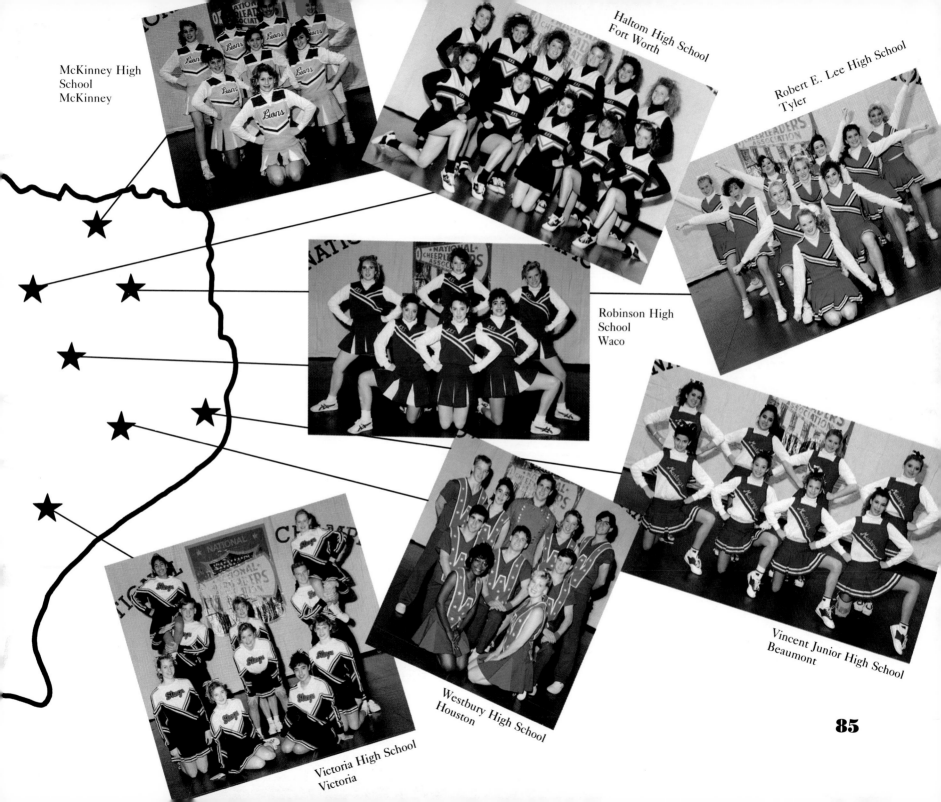

McKinney High
School
McKinney

Haltom High School
Fort Worth

Robert E. Lee High School
Tyler

Robinson High
School
Waco

Vincent Junior High School
Beaumont

Victoria High School
Victoria

Westbury High School
Houston

(courtesy: Debbi Blocker)

CHAPTER 7
DALLAS COWBOYS CHEERLEADERS
Cowgirls

(courtesy: Dallas Cowboys Cheerleaders)

During the summer of 1989, temperatures hovered around the hundred degree mark, making it unbearable for Dallasites to accomplish day-to-day necessities without complaining about the oppressive heat. The city that had never known true depression was also sweating from chapter eleven filings. Nationally renowned Southern Methodist University professor Ravi Batra predicted imminent monetary and mental collapse. It was during this, the worst economic disaster in Texas history, that affable Arkansas oilman Jerry Jones, a former University of Arkansas standout and longtime football fanatic, purchased the Dallas Cowboys.

Tempers flared, nerves shredded, and near exhaustion plagued these usually high-spirited Texans in the summer of 1989. Just when the soothsayers were predicting an economic bottoming out from this nightmare, the new kid on the block, Jones, soon to be barbecued by Texas sportswriters for terminal foot-in-mouth disease, fired his head coach. The unassuming Coach Tom Landry learned his fate on the ten o'clock news just like every other Joe in the world.

For most Texans this act was simply the straw that broke the camel's back. Public outrage was never so venomous. How dare Jones simply dismiss the beloved Landry, better known as the leader of "The God Squad." It was blasphemy. Jones instantly became the object of every Texan's frustration.

Then he tried to tamper with the Dallas Cowboys Cheerleaders. Citing that the cheerleaders' signature blue and white outfits were tired but true, he demanded that costume changes include spandex biker shorts and halter tops—something more akin to the Laker Girls' togs for which he was known to verbalize a personal preference. Not only that, but he wanted to lift the self-imposed cheerleader ban that prohibited the girls from appearing

Facing page: Sherri Brown, Miss May 1990, shows why the Dallas Cowboys Cheerleaders are considered the most photogenic professional cheerleaders in the world. *(courtesy: Dallas Cowboys Cheerleaders)*

All smiles as the Dallas Cowboys Cheerleaders pause before running into Texas Stadium. *(courtesy: J. Allen Hansley)*

Not all the action is on the 50-yard line. *(courtesy: J. Allen Hansley)*

Jumping out of white limos is a favorite field entrance for an entertainment half-time spectacular at Texas Stadium. *(courtesy: J. Allen Hansley)*

in uniform at functions where alcohol was served, stating that such sanctions were outdated and silly.

Hell hath no fury like that of a Texas woman scorned. It may not be nice to mess with Mother Nature, but offending the Dallas Cowboys Cheerleaders could actually constitute grounds for bodily harm. Unlike their southern belle sisters who would graciously wait for chivalrous lads to rise to their dueling defense, Texas women put on their war paint. Jones's scalp was to be their justice.

What many people may not have understood is that for quite some time, the Dallas Cowboys Cheerleaders have existed underneath the Dallas Cowboys organization. So, when Jones bought the Cowboys football team, in effect he bought the cheerleaders as well. He has always operated by his own version of the golden rule: "My gold, my rules." Though many changes were to be instituted in the Cowboys' game plan over the next several months, when the dust cleared, the cheerleaders would remain unscathed.

Autographing Dallas Cowboys Cheerleaders posters for fans, kids, and nursing home friends, whom many of the cheerleaders visit weekly. *(courtesy: J. Allen Hansley)*

90

The cheerleader controversy and ensuing soap opera played nightly on the national news and in every major daily newspaper in the country. Angry women flooded radio and television talk show lines with a defensive front that would make NOW jealous. Most of the current squad members defiantly walked off the squad rather than defer to such unacceptable defilation. Thousands of letters arrived daily in green duffle bags supporting the cheerleaders and echoing a now familiar cry: "Leave our cheerleaders alone!"

Rumors circulated in gossip columns that Dallas designer Victor Costa had been commissioned by Jones to create a new look for the squad, thus vaulting the whole mess into the international social arena. Though Costa confides that there were talks about new threads, he shrewdly admits that his sketches have since been conveniently misplaced or lost. It is likely that no one will ascertain what designs danced in Costa's dreams, but as the current darling of Seventh Avenue, he knew this cheerleader controversy was at best an albatross.

Cashing in on the controversy was the *Dallas Times Herald*, which mounted a campaign to redesign the Cowboys Cheerleaders' uniform with the aid of local designers. Narrowing the field down, the paper printed rough sketches of what new outfits might look like. None were met with wide-eyed approval. Multiples originator Sandra Garratt's designs appeared to be the front runner. The overwhelming consensus, however, indicated that the populace favored the current look. This was going to be more difficult than first envisioned.

Letters poured in from servicemen overseas who had watched the cheerleaders perform at Christmastime USO tours. Letters came from youngsters scrawling "Hang in

Want to make a Dallas Cowboys Cheerleaders fan angry? Suggest changing their blue and white outfits. Once considered risqué, these threads have been popular for almost twenty years. *(courtesy: J. Allen Hansley)*

Practice sessions at the Valley Ranch dance studio demand one's undivided attention. Eager alternates are ready to give their all if you don't. *(courtesy: J. Allen Hansley)*

there" on Big Chief notebook pads. Letters came on perfumed stationery from the many nursing home patients that the girls visit weekly in the Dallas–Fort Worth area. Dallas and the nation were concerned.

Jerry Jones, like many others around the country, was caught off guard by such affirmations of pom pon priority. He should have remembered that the Dallas Cowboys Cheerleaders was the nation's first professional cheerleading squad and the only one to have truly captured the hearts of all Americans, regardless of the Cowboys' winning habits. It has been the barometer by which all other professional cheerleading squads have measured their worth for the past twenty years.

The Houston Oilers' cheerleaders, called the Derrick Dolls, formed in the 1970s and rode the wave of success spawned by the Dallas cheerleaders. They never managed to find the right niche for their squad, however, and the organization finally folded in 1986 amid frustrations and lawsuits charging discriminatory selection processes. Veteran squad member Teresa Pettus confides that "as much as we don't want to admit it, the Dallas Cowboys Cheerleaders were better run and more popular than the Dolls. Houston was just too close to Dallas. The competition killed us."

Veteran Dallas Cowboy Cheerleaders director Suzanne Mitchell worked diligently for fourteen years, fiercely protecting her girls from tawdry exploitation and unnecessary commercialization. As part den mother and part drill sergeant, she, like Kilgore Rangerette maven Gussie Nell Davis, devoted the better part of her life to achieving success for her Dallas Cowboys Cheerleaders. It is a legacy that cheerleading fans throughout the world respect and support.

Messing with her girls is not tolerated. They have come a long way to reach their pinnacle of pom pon prowess. No one can tarnish the reputation they have worked long hours to establish and given their best energies to maintain.

When the Dallas Cowboys football organization was formed in 1960, even the most rabid pigskin fanatic was unprepared for the spell the professional jocks would cast over Dallas city life. Descending like a Trojan horse on the steps of City Hall, the Cowboys arrived in a placid era prior to the fatal overdose of Marilyn Monroe, the assassination of John F. Kennedy, and the social upheaval of the mid-1960s, which all but bypassed an economically charged Dallas.

Swashbuckling oil baron brothers John Murchison and Clint Murchison, Jr., founded the new football team, hiring a stoic Tom Landry as head coach. The Cowboys' image, real or imagined, reflected that of Landry: clean-cut, morally upright, and determined to win. But they were lacking a key ingredient: sideline support.

High school and college football in Texas had always enjoyed tremendously polished pom pon privilege. It therefore seemed natural to Tex Schramm, the Cowboys' new general manager, that the same notion would be embraced by the pro fans as well. Professional football was in its infancy in those pioneer days and the Cotton Bowl was rarely sold out. Though the verdict was still out on whether pro football would be a profitable venture, Schramm hired high school teacher Dee Brock to organize a group of models to double as cheerleaders, hoping to drum up the much-needed enthusiasm.

Brock argued that models, whom Schramm wanted to be by the sidelines, knew nothing about cheering and therefore would never sustain fan interest or survive the 120-plus-degree September heat on the AstroTurf. What Dee Brock did suggest was organizing a coed squad of Dallas–Fort Worth area high school students to lead cheers.

The high kick requires *daily* stretching and kicking to retain the limberness to perform well without pulling muscles. *(courtesy: J. Allen Hansley)*

Only the Dallas Cowboys Cheerleaders could successfully transform themselves into the roller darlings of the gridiron. *(courtesy: J. Allen Hansley)*

Originally billed as "Belles and Beaux," these thirty students marched out onto the sidelines as the original cheerleaders for the first Dallas Cowboys game. In exchange for trying to solicit crowd response, squad members received ten free tickets to Cowboys games.

It never occurred to Schramm or anyone else in Texas that football might be able to exist without the benefit of cheerleading. The fact was that the Cowboys was the only pro team commissioning pom pon action. This was Texas football, after all. Though these students were of the all-American Pepsi (or Coke) and apple pie generation, their efforts and collegiate-type cheers fell on deaf ears. Schramm discovered, though it was not a particularly astute observation, that pro football fans did not cheer their teams on as did college fans.

Moving to newly built Texas Stadium in 1971, Tex Schramm told Dee Brock that next year he wanted the most beautiful cheerleaders in the world to hit the AstroTurf along with his beloved Cowboys. He wanted them to dance like the Kilgore Rangerettes, the Apache Belles, the Dallas Tex Anns, and the Oak Cliff Golden Girls, who had all kicked and strutted their own brands of Texas flash at the Cowboys Cotton Bowl games. Sideline entertainment was to become the wave of the future, Schramm felt, and he wanted the best.

Dee Brock immediately contacted Dallas native Texie Waterman, who had been garnering rave reviews from her Broadway choreography. She became the first to bring New York–style jazz dancing to the fifty-yard line. With new midriff-baring uniforms designed by Dallasite Paula Van Waggoner, seven girls marched into the Texas Stadium spotlights in the fall of 1972 with the sexy look now associated with the current squad, and at last they were officially a squad of spirit leaders—the Dallas Cowboys Cheerleaders.

Though they were an instant hit with the fans, the

Texas news media complained that the cheerleaders were out on the field doing nothing more than bumps and grinds. They also guffawed when the Cowboys became the first team in the National Football League to obtain a registered trademark for its newly sewn cheerleader uniform. Against a barrage of criticism and unflattering barbs, new talent wasn't exactly breaking down the doors to try out in 1973, not like in 1990, when 1,500 girls from around the country lined up for the tryouts at Valley Ranch.

As NFL cameramen focused in on this new chorus line of Dallas dancers, millions of Sunday afternoon armchair quarterbacks scanned the screen trying to find the bouncing cheerleaders in compromising states of pom pon allurement. A heated debate erupted during the braless craze of the mid-1970s as to whether the Dallas Cowboys Cheerleaders indeed wore bras underneath those provocative halters. Press reports claimed they did not. NFL cameramen and color commentators always bragged of a story involving a never-to-be-confirmed incident of braless embarrassment.

The fact is that the cheerleaders have always been required to wear bras. Not suiting up properly is only one of a number of violations resulting in one having to turn in one's coveted blue and whites. The Dallas Cowboys Cheerleaders must have found it mildly amusing when a story appeared in the November 1988 issue of *Los Angeles* magazine detailing a day in the life of an L.A. Raiderette cheerleader. "Once in the middle of my routine, my blouse (sans bra) popped open. You can't stop, so you grab your pom pons and put them in front of you and dance," she told the writer.

"It could have never happened to us," says current Dallas Cowboys Cheerleader director and three-year veteran Leslie Haynes. "Our tops are not tied, they're stitched. They have not and will not ever come undone."

One will *never* spot squad members wearing rollers, chewing gum, smoking, or drinking once they exit their dressing rooms. *(courtesy: J. Allen Hansley)*

95

All Dallas Cowboys Cheerleaders like Helen Stubblefield accept choreographic direction during practice with eye contact and an enthusiastic "Thank you, Ma'am." *(courtesy: J. Allen Hansley)*

In a well-documented piece of film footage trivia at the 1976 Super Bowl, when a cheerleader innocently looked into the camera and winked to 75 million viewers, it vaulted the Dallas Cowboys Cheerleaders into superstardom. Television had discovered the next darlings of the screen, much in the same manner that Farrah Fawcett was spotted in the stands at a University of Texas football game. Overnight sensations, these pistol-packing cheer masters became the hot pants darlings of the camera, creating a phenomenon soon to steal thunder from the football field itself. The Dallas Cowboys Cheerleaders became the heartthrob of every male viewer and the envy of every housewife.

Fusing provocative outfits, dangerous curves, and a childlike innocence, the Cowboys Cheerleaders hit the jackpot in the Nielsen ratings. While other professional squads were struggling to update their groups from the stripper-waitress-actress-model-dancer mold, the Dallas Cowboys Cheerleaders paraded a lineup as squeaky clean as Tom Landry's closet. Many of these girls were former high school cheerleaders, stewardesses, legal secretaries, or even white-collar professionals. Unlike their compatriots in other locales, they were the undisputed stars of the city. The hit of every posh party, they were showered with adoration at every turn.

Suzanne Mitchell required the girls to practice three to four hours each day, Monday through Friday, as well as undergo a grueling summer training session. They had to be in shape in order to wear the revealing outfits and dance the newest jazz steps from Texie Waterman. Painstaking controls were shackled on the girls' professional and private lives so that the reputation of the squad and that of the organization would remain impeccable. There was to be no scandal and no tarnish. Most of the squad members are former beauty pageant contestants.

Rules of the organization are simple and to the point. Cheerleaders must wear their uniforms only to Dallas Cowboys Cheerleaders–approved events, never in private, and they must be turned back in upon leaving the group. The girls must wear their uniform to each game, arriving two hours before kick off. No hair curlers, gum, alcohol, or cigarettes are allowed while in uniform. With the exception of tiny stud earrings and a Cowboys Cheerleaders ring, no jewelry is to be worn.

Missing a rehearsal prior to a game means staying on the sidelines for that particular game. All must sign a one-year exclusive modeling contract with the Dallas Cowboys organization that prohibits them from participating in any modeling or commercial work outside the Dallas Cowboys Cheerleaders arena. Acting roles fall under the same category. All interviews with the women must be conducted at cheerleaders' Valley Ranch offices, and under no circumstances are reporters, among others, allowed to contact girls at home. Any fraternization with the Cowboys football players is grounds for immediate dismissal.

Squad members are required to address superiors with a bright "Yes, ma'am" or "Thank you, ma'am." Bras are worn as a part of their uniform.

Riding a wave of popularity never before granted to cheerleaders of any type, the fall of 1978 kicked off the filming of one of television's biggest ratings sweeps gimmicks: *The Dallas Cowboys Cheerleaders.* Producer Bob Hamner got the idea watching the women on Sunday afternoon football, thinking, "Hey, these girls would make a great made-for-television movie." He was right. It's hard to imagine that just a few short years before, the press jabbed the women at every turn. They had gone to Hollywood to make movies. The world was now their oyster.

Dallas Cowboys Cheerleaders are groomed to be the most camera savvy of any cheerleaders in the world. *(courtesy: J. Allen Hansley)*

97

Alona Wood demonstrates the power of the pom pon. *(courtesy: J. Allen Hansley)*

Then the December 1978 *Playboy* hit the stands. Ex-"Charlie's Angels" star Farrah Fawcett was on the cover. The centerfold was a woman from Austin. But the real interest was in a section entitled "Texas Cowgirls, Inc." Former Dallas Cowboys Cheerleader Tina Jiminez found squad regulations (like *no* appearances at the Dallas Playboy Club) a step behind the times. Not making the squad in 1977, she proceeded to form her own renegade posse called Texas Cowgirls, Inc., which would pop out of cakes in similarly designed blue and white outfits. Some of the women who posed for the revealing *Playboy* pictorial were former and current Cowboys Cheerleaders. It was Suzanne Mitchell's worst nightmare.

There was, as one would expect, a major flap. Any squad members baring all were of course asked to turn in their uniforms. Women in the squad felt violated in a weird, media sort of way. The fact that *Playboy* had tried to upstage their forthcoming movie hurt them, despite the fact that all would soon be forgotten. The movie remains as the seventh-highest-rated television movie in history, commanding a successful follow-up: *Dallas Cowboys Cheerleaders II*.

Though Jiminez and her expatriots soon disbanded and faded into obscurity, their fifteen minutes of fame has, unfortunately, dogged the cheerleaders since. Jiminez coined the term *Cowgirls*; *Playboy* gave them the space. Innocuous though it seemed at first, the phrase has stuck with the Dallas Cowboys Cheerleaders. If one wants to ruffle feathers, innocently walk into the cheerleaders' office and ask Haynes about the Cowgirls. Do so at a safe distance, however. It is a subject that is never discussed. *Never.* Haynes immediately will move on to the more pressing issues at hand. Rightfully so. Every year, she schedules more than two hundred appearances, organizes several USO tours, polishes any camera-wise rough edges, and fiercely defends and protects her

Facing page: Overseas holiday USO tours present the girls in star-spangled extravaganzas displaying vocal, dramatic, and toe-tapping talents. *(courtesy: Dallas Cowboys Cheerleaders)*

women in the Mitchell tradition. Just to obtain an interview with several of her cheerleaders takes an act of Congress.

Director Leslie Haynes sorts through the more than one thousand pieces of fan mail arriving weekly at her Valley Ranch office as well as oversees the more than five hundred weekly handwritten responses from the cheerleaders. Haynes, like her predecessor, turns down thousands of requests annually for marketing ideas and commercial endorsements, because few in such an industry will allow her complete control—the only way she legally can protect her girls. Ironically, this has contributed to a lack of consumer burnout; therefore, the cheerleaders have consistently maintained a high level of consumer interest that seemingly never wanes.

As the squad has grown into its own persona, it has smoothly woven itself into the city's social whirl along with cast members from the hit TV series "Dallas." Nowhere else in the country have cheerleaders and actors been so embraced by the upper crust, the media, and the paparazzi. Dallas loves them. They are the epitome of good, clean sexiness, a star-spangled Sunday afternoon extravaganza fittin' to watch in one's Sunday clothes.

For all their blood, sweat, and fears, the cheerleaders are paid $15 a game . . . before taxes. All just for the chance to suit up in those blue and whites.

"I feel different when I put on my uniform," says Dallas Cowboys Cheerleader rookie Carrie Blanke. As a member of the world's most famous cheerleader lineup of all time, she is probably right. To see Carrie off the field, one would assume that she was another beautiful coed at the University of Texas at Arlington. But when she straps on the legendary uniform, she simply transforms.

Barely nineteen years old, she was born the same year that the Dallas Cowboys Cheerleaders officially began.

The cheerleaders have been superstars for as long as she has been alive. For many on the squad, like Carrie, the ambition to become a Dallas Cowboys Cheerleader is not one of prime-time exposure, the chance for fame, or the possibility of being "discovered," as many outsiders may assume. The statistics bear this out. Few have used the group as a springboard to so-called higher destinies.

As one Dallas Cowboys Cheerleader told me, "We work so hard for the chance to wear a uniform that we cannot take with us when we leave. But once you've worn that uniform, you really never take it off. You just give it to someone else."

Is it the magic in the uniform or the mystery inside the women that gives them a seemingly mystical effervescence? No one will ever know. It's one of the great affirmations of the Texas cosmos. Only those who wear the uniform know.

Enthusiasm must be projected to the top row of Texas Stadium. (courtesy: J. Allen Hansley)

A half-time show is not complete without good ole Texas high kicks. *(courtesy: J. Allen Hansley)*

Facing page: The 1991 Dallas Cowboys Cheerleaders poster original hangs in Jerry Jones' office, owner of the Dallas Cowboys. *(courtesy: Dallas Cowboys Cheerleaders)*

102

CHAPTER 8
ALL THAT
BIZ
The Selling of Yelling

(courtesy: J. Allen Hansley)

103

(courtesy: National Cheerleaders Association)

(courtesy: National Cheerleaders Association)

As a teenager, Lawrence Herkimer would leave his home on Abbott Street and walk down the railroad tracks to North Dallas High School, where he faced his stuttering problem every day. Ironically, as he walked down those rails, he discovered that he developed balance and, subsequently, muscle control. Surely he could do the same with his stuttering problem, he concluded. So he bravely enrolled in a speech class.

He soon learned that his speech problem could be controlled, but only with a lot of practice. The confidence he gained from that speech teacher enabled him to put his burgeoning gymnastic flipness to good use. He tried out for high school cheerleader and his individual popularity snagged him a squad position first time out, therein making an amazing discovery: he never stuttered when he cheered.

"If people had told me back then that I would be making my living going around the country lecturing on cheerleading, I would have never believed them, because I couldn't speak worth a darn," laughs the sixty-four-year-old Herkimer. "I did overcome it. The only thing now is that I really can't put on a subterfuge 'cause I start to stutter. I guess it's God's way of making me an honest man."

After college in 1948, Lawrence Herkimer, whose philosophy was "I think I can, I think I can," opened a fledgling company called National Cheerleaders Association in his hometown of Dallas. If not for the help of his wife's teaching job, they would have starved during the initial twelve months. However, over the forty-odd years of their existence, things happened. In 1991, combined annual sales from cheerleader camps, supplies, and uniforms now exceeded the $50 million mark. More important, though, Herkimer changed the American sports scene forever, and Texas cheerleaders became his prototype.

(courtesy: National Cheerleaders Association)

(courtesy: J. Allen Hansley)

Few believed that the enthusiastic former Southern Methodist University head cheerleader had any future in the business of yelling. Granted, he was one of the first to introduce flips and gymnastic stunts into the cheerleading scene in the post–World War II era of ankle skirts and saddle oxfords. His mother often was overheard saying that just once she would like to see an upright photo of her son. Herkie was rebuked many times: it was OK to have one's head in the clouds so long as one's feet were planted firmly on the ground. "Get a real job," folks told him.

Herkie ignored the conventional wisdom that surrounded him and organized the first cheerleader camp in history at Huntsville's Sam Houston State University in the early 1950s. C. R. Hackney, head of the university's music department, believed in Herkie's idea enough to bring him down for a five-day summer clinic,

(courtesy: National Cheerleaders Association)

rounding out the cast with a speech professor to present tips on speaking in front of an audience and an English teacher to aid with cheer rhymes. Neither the English nor the speech teacher impressed the fifty-two girls who attended the seminar, but Herkie did. He used gymnastics and vigorous cheer movements to show them how to stimulate and direct crowd response. The girls were elated. They had experienced a totally innovative phenomenon.

The following year, Herkie convinced Hackney not to invite the stuffy profs in lieu of cheerleaders from Rice and Baylor, both of whom were recent Herkie converts. The three preached the Gospel according to Herkie to the two hundred fresh-faced girls, and it became evident that Herkie had found his niche. Continuing in that same tradition in 1990, his philosophy was absorbed by more than 150,000 students in 385 camps conducted in every state in the union except Rhode Island and in foreign markets, including Japan, New Zealand, Germany, Colombia, Ireland, England, and Australia.

True notoriety gripped Herkie when others tagged his personal high-flying jump as the "Herkie." His signature jump was simply the way Herkie vaulted himself into free-form. Punching the right fist vertically in the air with the left hand planted firmly on the hip, the left leg thrusts forward with the right leg tucked underneath in a sort of midair split. From the stands, the Herkie appears to be an easy maneuver suspended at the apex, but it is not so. More difficult stunts do exist, but none capture the true spirit of cheerleading any more, and it remains the only namesake cheerleading jump.

Shortly after establishing his camps, Herkimer traveled to New York and stumbled upon a new electronic contraption called the television set. Realizing that the little chrome batons that majorettes twirled on Texas turf would be virtually unrecognizable from grandstand

(courtesy: National Cheerleaders Association)

cameras, he came up with the idea of tying vividly colored crepe paper streamers on a little stick that could be waved in the air to attract attention. This was the birth of the pom pon. Choreographed to the tune of "Lollipop," the Wichita, Texas, high school cheerleaders made history as the first troupe to perform a halftime routine using these new hand-held props.

It was actually Herkimer's wife, Dorothy, who nudged him into his next sister company, Cheerleader Supply Company. ("You can't do back flips forever, hon.") After his day at NCA and her day teaching school, the two would head to their garage to package pom pon kits to sell to area high school cheerleaders. Although these days were lean, Dorothy denies ever having sewn a cheerleader uniform, as has been erroneously reported over the years. "Couldn't ever sew a lick," she says. But she does admit to having worked her fingers to the bone assembling pom pon kits.

Crepe paper was not the sturdiest for pom pons. It faded, tore, and, worst yet, bled and disintegrated when wet. That was before vinyl, and no other options existed until the 1960s, when Houston's Perma Pom began manufacturing both vinyl and plastic pom pons for Cheerleader Supply. Nonetheless, pom pon popularity soared despite their inherent messiness. No Texas cheerleader was without pom pons by the mid-1950s.

Most don't realize that the word *pom-pom* should actually be *pompon*. Herkimer was in the midst of his first Hawaiian cheerleader clinic when he unknowingly committed his first major pom faux pas. He was on stage in front of thousands of enthusiastic islanders when he announced that he was going to demonstrate a "pom-pom" routine. Instantly, unison gasps quieted a previously responsive audience and a hush fell over the crowd.

The man who started it all, Lawrence Herkimer, addresses the crowd at the 1990 cheerleader nationals prior to presenting the winning trophies. NCA's army of instructors stands at attention in the background. *(courtesy: J. Allen Hansley)*

"Don't you have pom-pom girls over here?" Herkimer asked timidly, unsure of what was happening. Charging onto the stage, the school principal whispered to Herkimer that "pom-pom" had a negative connotation. "We don't use *that* word over here."

Recalling his former navy days in the Philippines, Herkimer flashed back on natives yelling at servicemen: "Hey, Joe, wanna pom-pom my sister?" Whoa! The spelling was immediately changed to *pom pon*—two words, one M, one N.

With Cheerleader Supply in full swing in the 1950s offering pleated pretties for every occasion, Herkimer realized that students needed a venue by which to help pay for the perky new threads. Unlike today's generation, very few held after-school jobs in those days, and those who did usually toed the mark for family-owned businesses or farms and were unaccustomed to receiving compensation.

Opposed to the likes of those who made the rounds selling candy, light bulbs, and candles, Herkimer demanded a combination sales product that coincidentally bolstered school spirit, and he came up with it in the form of the booster ribbon. Starting with "Beat the Bears" or some facsimile thereof, the money-making items were soon to include ribbons for basketball as well as those for football, megaphones, score cards, mascot-printed miniature footballs, booster buttons, and souvenir pennants, all sold at low price points. These items paved the way for cheerleaders to afford cheer camps or spirit uniforms. You name it, and Cheerleader Supply makes it. For many, this meant that cheerleader heaven was within reach.

In the 1970s, pom pon paradise rattled when several of Herkie's longtime employees and former devotees packed their bags with his ideas and headed for Memphis, Tennessee, to form their own competing cheerleader dynasty, Universal Cheerleaders Association (UCA). Their defection remains a thorn in the side of those loyal to NCA. Initially, the band of renegades was treated with disdain by their former compatriots and cheer groups, as if they had committed an unpardonable sin. Herkie and NCA had weathered cheer competition before from other organizations, mainly on the West Coast, but this insiders' sellout (at least in NCA's eyes) cut deep and has yet to heal.

Part of their disagreement surrounded the growing demand for cheerleader competition, a school of thought fiercely rejected by NCA and its staff until the 1980s. But the synchronized cheering and gymnastically riveting routines now incorporated by NCA as standard cheer procedure cajoled its subjects into substandard cheer competitions elsewhere, thus resulting in many a sprained muscle or broken bone.

Texas cheerleaders were not content to watch the teams they supported continue to be rated weekly in the sports sections while their squads had no tangible route for similar rankings. Why should football and basketball teams be the only ones worthy of state or national rankings? Then the unthinkable occurred. Some cheerleading squads defected to UCA or other smaller cheer organizations that conducted annual competitions. Texans are extremely competitive by nature. They demanded to have their chance to prove that they are the best.

Resisting this urge for several years by preaching the inherent faults and physical dangers of such competitive gatherings, Herkimer became extremely frustrated by the increasingly dangerous lack of justifiable controls sanctioned by these so-called splinter groups. The contests seemed to focus strictly on which squad could perform the most intricate routine, with no guidelines for safety or true spirit leading. Pyramids stacked two-high

(courtesy: National Cheerleaders Association)

the first year, three-high the next year, and three-high with a back flip off the top the following. Herkimer saw danger in all of this exploitation. His cheerleaders were being led down the wrong path; something had to be done quickly or the powers that be would soon outlaw cheerleading because such wild stunts were growing out of control.

The 1980s became the decade of NCA's National Cheerleader Competitions. Herkimer, along with husband-and-wife team Lance and Carol Wagers, devised a comprehensive plan of action. If they were to sponsor and sanction cheer competitions, there would have to be rigid standards for each age group designating restrictions for pyramid height, acceptable flips and stunts, choreography and length of routine, and spotters, and a panel of impartial judges would need to be established. The result was that the NCA, the nation's most respected cheer organization, established itself as the nation's most respected organizer of cheer competition.

UCA then hit NCA with a one-two punch by becoming the first cheer competition to be aired nationally on ESPN. The two-hour show, originating from Florida's Sea World, is so popular that it is aired numerous times throughout the year. Many even assume that when they watch the show they are indeed looking at the NCA nationals. Needless to say, this does not sit well at NCA's office. Texans do not like to be upstaged.

Additionally, one of Herkimer's biggest supporters, Loyce Bates, a longtime NCA adviser, switched her University of Texas cheerleaders from NCA to UCA for the 1990 competition. Though neither has anything but the kindest words for the other, one could feel the sense of betrayal by the NCA staffers at the 1990 NCA finals without the Longhorn squad. "We'll get them back," seemed to be the general consensus.

Though chapter eleven bankruptcies are common in

post-oil-crunch Texas these days, most were stunned when NCA filed for protection under chapter eleven early in 1990. It's an intricate tale of another leveraged buyout gone bad. "We should have never had to file bankruptcy," says a kindly Herkimer, shaking his head, still not believing the action himself.

In 1986, Herkimer sold Cheerleader Supply and the association to BSN, a Dallas-based sportswear manufacturer, for $13 million and BSN stock. BSN grouped the two organizations with similar companies, forming National Spirit. Herkimer stayed on as chief executive officer. Then BSN sold National Spirit to the Prospect Group, a company with diverse interests, for $46 million, along with $2.5 million reinvested by Herkimer. That's when the new troubles began. Through a series of aboveboard financial dealings involving the basic paper shuffle, National Spirit defaulted on debt service, throwing everything into a mess. Though none of the companies involved were in jeopardy of closing shop, it took several months before arrangements could be finalized to set Herkimer's baby back on track. Just in time for summer camps to roll around.

The business of yelling. No one, not even Herkimer himself, could have foreseen such an empire built on enthusiasm. Organizing thousands of the nation's best cheerleaders to march, he has them parading not only in Texas, but in such faraway places as New York; Dublin, Ireland; London, Great Britain; Tokyo, Japan; and in hundreds of other pageantry locations. He employs staff uniform designers, media consultants, cheer advisers, and runs hundreds of camps and clinics, and can supply cheerleading paraphernalia for every occasion under the sun—that's a long way from his first clinic at Sam Houston State University in the late 1940s.

NCA's fashion staff will tailor a uniform to meet a squad's specifications. Shown here in competition are the Corsicana High School cheerleaders. *(courtesy: J. Allen Hansley)*

NCA cheerleaders loose balloons during the 1989 Macy's Thanksgiving Day Parade in tribute to spirit leaders everywhere. *(courtesy: National Cheerleaders Association)*

CHAPTER 9
DRILLING IN TEXAS

(courtesy: Tyler Junior College)

Nobody stands a straighter line than the Kilgore Rangerettes. *(courtesy: Kilgore College)*

This cover of *The Saturday Evening Post*, October 5, 1963, belonged to the Kilgore Rangerettes. They have also graced the covers of *Life* and *Esquire* magazines. *(courtesy: The Saturday Evening Post)*

"We're *not* cheerleaders, young man, so you promise me that you'll think about changing the title of this book before I'll even think about talking to you," a perturbed Gussie Nell Davis crackled. Evidently I had struck a raw nerve. The feisty eighty-five-year-old founder of the legendary Kilgore Rangerettes has spent most of her life devoted to Texas drill teams. She didn't achieve world-class fame by sitting demurely on the sidelines or taking unintentional insults from "young whippersnappers" like myself.

There is a definitive difference between cheerleaders who lead yells and dance or drill team members who march and kick above their heads, but we tend to lump them all together. It really irks Davis, no doubt.

Years ago, *Esquire* magazine couldn't seem to get anything right. In a big photo spread, the editors erroneously identified the Rangerette captains as not only "Boomer Sooner cheerleaders [but] the pride of Oklahoma." Talk about not fact-checking. Lividness might be considered a mild term for the holy terror Davis unleashed on "those idiots in New York City." The humble editors promptly reran the original photo in a later issue, blazing a huge "apology" across the top of the full-page spread: "*Esquire* apologizes to the Mayor and citizens of Kilgore, Texas, for the above captioned error. We compliment the students of Kilgore College on having such pretty cheerleaders. *Esquire* should have known such beautiful girls could only have come from the state of Texas." Davis rolls her eyes. The pages are boldly framed in the Rangerettes' head office.

Her interest was never cheering. "Dancing, my dear. It was always dancing." When growing up in Farmersville, Texas, hometown to Audie Murphy, if one danced, one got thrown out of church. "Too many Baptists and Church of Christ types whose halos are on too tight," she's said. "Cuts off circulation to the brain.

"Beauty Knows No Pain" is the Kilgore Rangerettes' motto. A frown never crosses their face when in uniform. *(courtesy: Kilgore College)*

KILGORE COLLEGE
Rangerettes

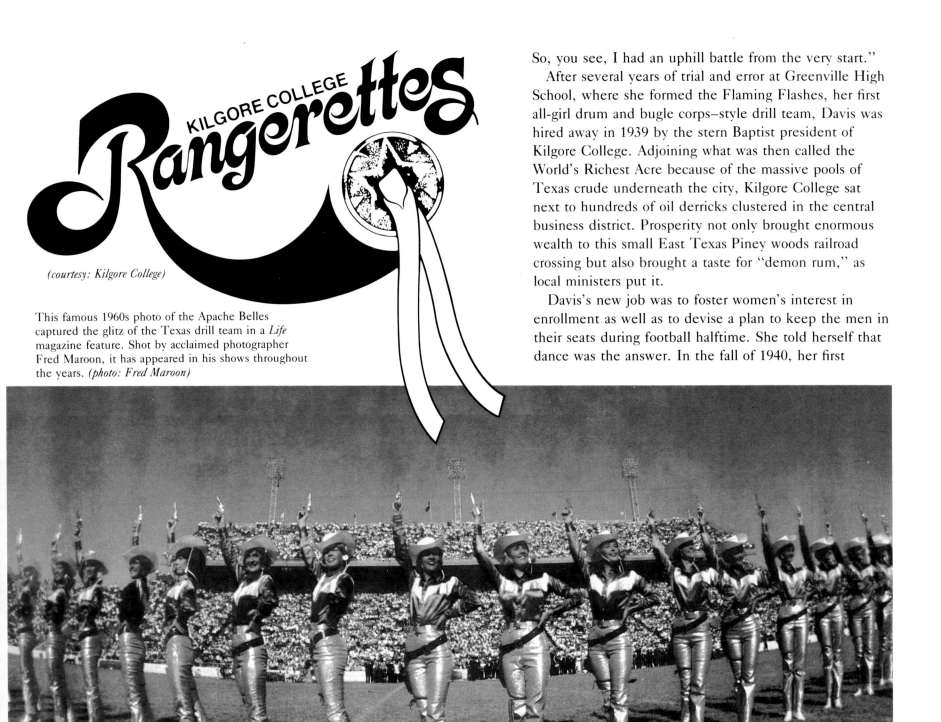

(courtesy: Kilgore College)

This famous 1960s photo of the Apache Belles captured the glitz of the Texas drill team in a *Life* magazine feature. Shot by acclaimed photographer Fred Maroon, it has appeared in his shows throughout the years. *(photo: Fred Maroon)*

So, you see, I had an uphill battle from the very start."

After several years of trial and error at Greenville High School, where she formed the Flaming Flashes, her first all-girl drum and bugle corps–style drill team, Davis was hired away in 1939 by the stern Baptist president of Kilgore College. Adjoining what was then called the World's Richest Acre because of the massive pools of Texas crude underneath the city, Kilgore College sat next to hundreds of oil derricks clustered in the central business district. Prosperity not only brought enormous wealth to this small East Texas Piney woods railroad crossing but also brought a taste for "demon rum," as local ministers put it.

Davis's new job was to foster women's interest in enrollment as well as to devise a plan to keep the men in their seats during football halftime. She told herself that dance was the answer. In the fall of 1940, her first

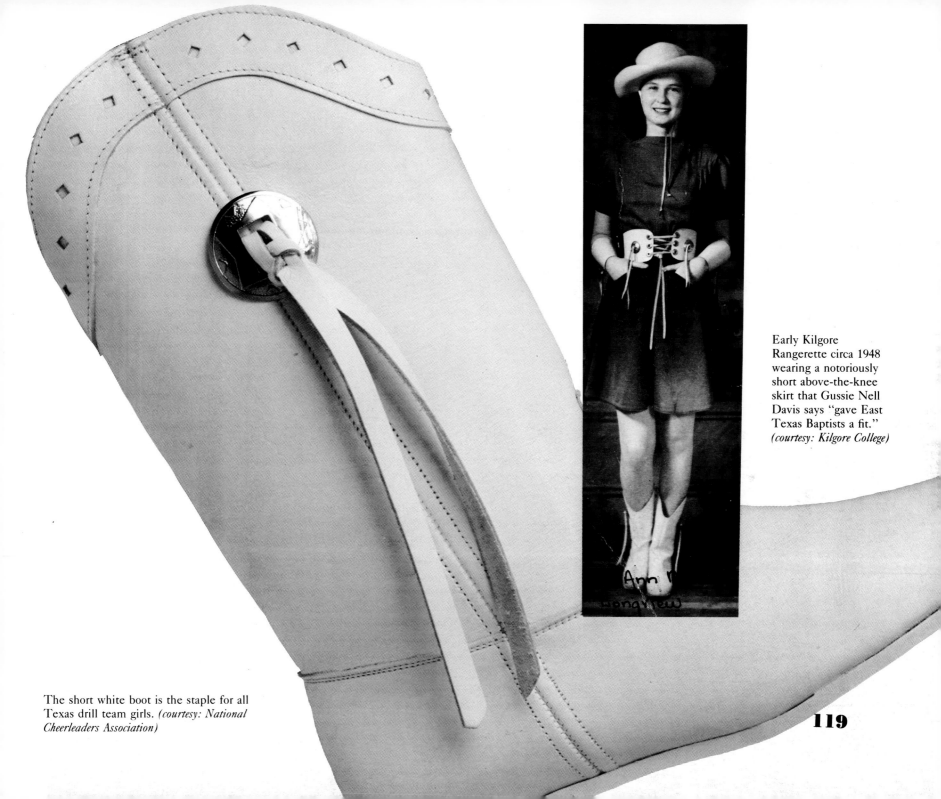

Early Kilgore Rangerette circa 1948 wearing a notoriously short above-the-knee skirt that Gussie Nell Davis says "gave East Texas Baptists a fit." *(courtesy: Kilgore College)*

The short white boot is the staple for all Texas drill team girls. *(courtesy: National Cheerleaders Association)*

119

Drill team ambassadors to the world. *(courtesy: Kilgore College)*

halftime show included a fireworks display, precision military marching, and a few waist-high kicks from belles in white western hats and red, white, and blue outfits whose scandalously short skirts barely touched the knees. Halftimers never saw the underside of the bleachers again.

The precisional diva brought show business thrills to the fifty-yard line, introducing the world's most celebrated high kickers and creating a truly unique American art form called the drill team. Davis is credited with introducing the most famous drill team step of all time, the contagion, where motions ripple down the line of girls and back again, with split-second precision and fluidness. Drill team extravaganzas in the last sixty years are a result of her ability to fuse dance, high kicks, and colorful props, such as flags, streamers, beach balls, ladders, or wooden oil derricks. The world feasted their eyes on those leggy Texas gals.

Surprisingly, the general assumption that the Rangerettes performed their traditional high kick from inception is incorrect. "At first, the girls kicked just above waist high," relates current director Deana Bolton. "Miss Davis probably won't tell you this, but we didn't start kicking really high until 1960." At the time, Bolton, a former national baton champion, directed a drill team called the Dallas Tex Anns, which performed at the Dallas Texans pro football games. The professional team that shared Dallas with the Dallas Cowboys eventually headed north, reincarnating as the Kansas City Chiefs. Davis came to visit her longtime friend Deana Bolton and to watch her Tex Anns routines at the Cotton Bowl. Also on the program were the Oak Cliff (Dallas) Golden Girls, a self-styled Rockettes-type group dressed in flashy top hats, tails, and seamed hose.

"I said, *look* Miss Davis [yes, they really call each other Miss so-and-so], see how high they're kicking? Way above their heads!"

(courtesy: Kilgore College)

121

The high kick meets the fast kick. The Kilgore Rangerettes go backstage at Radio City Music Hall to pose with the Rockettes. *(courtesy: Kilgore College)*

"We'll be kicking that way tomorrow, only better," Davis replied. They have ever since.

Davis is a perfectionist and not one to mince words: "I was hard as nails on my girls," she says in one of her standard quotes. "By the time I got through with them, they were either scared to death to act like heathens or just too tired." *Perfection* is the key word to the success of drill teams like the Rangerettes.

Other drill team enthusiasts were eager to duplicate her success, right down to her high kicks and insistence that the girls perform with the school band, *never* to recorded music. "Copy cats," Davis says. Imitation *is* the sincerest form of flattery, Miss Davis. Her stiffest competition was to come from Tyler Junior College, twenty-eight miles down the road. Though the people in Tyler probably don't want to admit it, Apache Belle founder Mildred Stringer was hired in 1947 to organize a drill team to best their neighboring rival. The first Apache Belle uniforms were fringed Native American costumes of brown cotton to simulate buckskin. But, unlike the Rangerettes, whose uniforms have effectively never changed except for skirt length, the Apache Belles have had numerous costume transformations, most recently emerging in black spandex and fringe.

Competition for bragging rights was and always will be fierce. Both groups have traveled around the world and been featured in almost every major bowl game or television show. The Rangerettes have performed consecutively in the Cotton Bowl since 1951, appeared on the "Ed Sullivan Show" and "60 Minutes" and on the covers of *Life*, *Esquire*, and the *Saturday Evening Post*, and were featured in the films *Beauty Knows No Pain* (though somewhat unflatteringly according to Bolton) and *Seven Wonders of the World*, in which they were acknowledged as the eighth wonder.

The Apache Belles, who have made similar, though

122

less frequent, bowl appearances, joined Kenny Rogers on stage, strutted their stuff at the Texas Rose Festival, and surprised even Los Angeles critics by being featured in David Byrne's highly acclaimed movie *True Stories*. The only group of Texas spirit leaders snagging more television airtime than these two groups are none other than the ever-popular Dallas Cowboys Cheerleaders, at whom Davis often fires carefully aimed potshots: "They're neither cheerleaders nor a precision drill team. I'm a lady or I'd really tell you what I call them."

Trading barbs seems to consume more energy among drill team members than cheerleaders, for some inexplicable reason. "Poochie bellies, that's what we used to call them," says Louise Sevier Hughes, a former Rangerette turned Atlanta socialite. "But that's OK. They used to call us Raunchyettes."

Current Apache Belle director Ruth Flynn has been fortunate to share the excitement of both teams. As a former Rangerette, she met some stiff opposition when she took the helm at Tyler Junior College in 1986. Because the two groups mix like water and oil, former Apache Belles doubted her sincerity as much as former Rangerettes felt betrayed, as though she might be selling secrets to the enemy.

Don't sell Flynn short, though. Don't ever sell a Texas woman short. Living in the shadow of her Kilgore rivals may not be easy, but she presents a first-rate show.

Despite enormous popularity, drill teams, however, never established themselves in Texas's four-year institutions. ("It's a junior college thing," admits Gussie Nell Davis.) Cheerleaders were the main attraction. Some muse that because the Rangerettes emerged from a little-known junior college, universities simply were not interested. Besides, they had big-time athletic programs hogging the spotlight. Others theorize that the lack of highly visible cheerleaders on the junior college level

The Cotton Bowl crowd roared as the Apache Belles marched onto the field in electrifying gold lame Western outfits. *(photo: Fred Maroon)*

123

The pizazz of the Apache Belles is a hard act to follow in 1990. *(courtesy: Tyler Junior College)*

paved the way for high kicker prominence, filling a void.

By the late 1950s, drill team hysteria had reached such proportions that most every high school and junior college in the state had the precision-popping females smiling and high-kicking their way into hearts everywhere. Because Texans have never embraced the traditional pep squad as they have been in other southern states, the drill team is *everything*. In larger schools, sections of the football stadiums are set aside just to seat the drill team. Not making the team as a sophomore was enough to send the disgraced into blatant weeping, wailing, and gnashing of teeth. It truly is not uncommon for the outcasts to beg parents for private school privilege, where one may be able to hide such shame.

An unexpected slump hit during the 1970s. Partly due to post-Vietnam apathy compounded by a thrust of cheerleader muscle, interest among high schoolers in these highly disciplined groups hit an all-time low. School sponsors were begging girls to try out, but with little success. Former drill team numbers shrank considerably, leaving those hangers-on feeling like ugly stepsisters compared to their pom pon siblings, all of whom were busy basking in their televised glory. They could no longer prance with pride.

The uniforms were too hot, old-fashioned, even corny, they whined. The regimentation was too restrictive, armylike, and physically demanding. In August, one had to fight the 100-plus-degree heat, sand burs, and the dreaded fire ants. November's wind sliced right through to the bone. Nearing exhaustion in the late 1970s, drill teams suddenly got their second wind and, like cheerleaders, they caught the spirit of spirit leading.

Seemingly overnight, a new band of drill team enthusiasts emerged. Gussie Nell Davis protégées materialized everywhere and demanded the respect they deserved. New outfits, new attitude. Even the measly

124

$1,200 yearly stipend for the drill coach, just like their cheer coach rivals, didn't deter enthusiasm. Drill teams with the right stuff decided to give cheerleaders a run for their money. Their weapon was none other than dance. Davis had known it all along.

Drill team aficionados can expect two distinct drill philosophies, best described as the petticoat versus spandex. To those in spandex, the petticoats are old-fashioned, underdisciplined, outdated, uninteresting, unfit to do anything but stand at field attention and look pretty. The petticoats counter that the spandexers are overachieving Stepford students spending too much time on their wiggle, not enough on formations, and too much money on pricey camps and unnecessary outfits. Both agree that dance is the move with the groove. Now if they could just agree on which dance.

The division is no more evident than in Dallas, where drill team members have been known to outnumber the Longhorn Band. To the petticoats like the Woodrow Wilson High School Sweethearts, all of this dance and recorded music threatens their very existence of polished white leather boots, dusted tilted derby, spotless double-faced gloves, and starched underwear. They really don't care about the shimmy shakedown or pom pons. They like their more casual approach to practice, regimented formations, and the fact that the outfits can be passed down. They fiercely defend their performance levels, saying, "Leave the Paula Abdul moves to the cheerleaders."

The flip side to this philosophy are the Hillcrest High School Panaders. Practice begins at 7:00 A.M. sharp under the direction of an ambitious new director, Julie Groth. Their sleek and sexy look is more combination high steppers and Laker Girls than traditional drill team, but it does not bother those sweating in shimmering neon body suits, trying to perfect a new routine before first

Like mother, like daughter. Meredith Oden, age 4, hopes to follow in her mom's footsteps to become a Kilgore Rangerette. Kim Chapman Oden of Garland, Texas, dressed Meredith up as a tribute to the group's Fiftieth anniversary in 1989. *(courtesy: Kim Chapman Oden)*

125

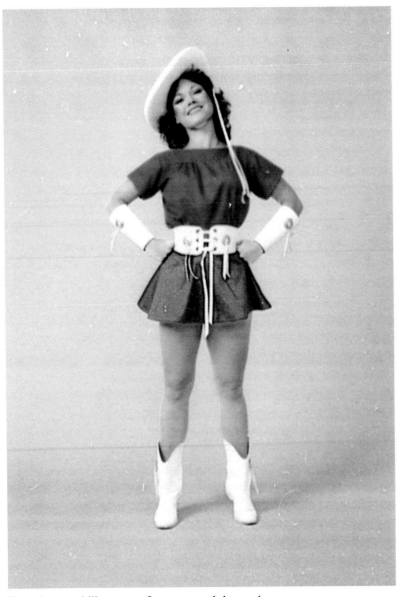

Though most drill team outfits are passed down, the item most girls want to take with them is their hat.
(*courtesy: Kilgore College*)

period. They consider themselves a dance team more than a traditional drill team like the Sweethearts, and a good one at that. Those who don't abide by the rules are issued demerits. Accumulate enough, and an eager alternate will jump into your tights before they're out of the dryer.

Not everyone believes in drill teams. Several Texas high school principals, preferring anonymity, confess that drill teams are by far their worst headache of the year. The anguish transcends the now-expected August phone calls from irate parents whose darlings have not been named captain. In Texas, squads are considered small if only suiting one hundred. By comparison, most drill teams outside Texas number between thirty and forty girls. The sheer numbers are mind boggling for those trying to organize the performance dates or just to move the girls along with their costumes, hats, and frills from the school to an off-site football stadium and back. It's become overemphasized, they claim, but it is the kids who demand it.

Jeannie Smith has been training girls for the past thirty-five years at her suburban Dallas studio. She teaches dance, baton twirling, and drill structure, starting for many at age three and continuing through high school. I can already hear screams of the ill-informed "don't understands" charging child manipulation solely to satisfy a parent's own secret longings of drill respect. Maybe, for a limited few. But if kids can worm their way out of unwanted piano lessons, they can do the same thing with the drill team. A quick reality check tells us that Texas girls *love* being involved in drill teams. It's not conscription, they *want* it. In Texas, that's good enough reason for anyone.

No matter one's age, there's a magical something about being a little girl in Texas and strutting your stuff in flashy costumes that is sooooooo Texan. And it's something we all love to watch.

Dance and drill are here to stay, according to Joyce Pennington, founder of Dance/Drill Team Directors of America and president of the American Drill Team School, one of several Texas companies that host nationally respected camps and on-site workshops. She believes, like Gussie Nell Davis, that whether it be the high kick or the body rock, like she choreographs for the Dallas Mavericks (pro basketball) Dancers, dance is here to stay.

Conducting summer camps that annually train more than 10,000 drill teamers, half of them Texans, Pennington also offers peewee classes for seven-year-olds. Just like her cheer counterparts, she cannot form classes fast enough to satisfy the drill hungry, no matter the age. "Drill and dance teams are finally coming of age for the mainstream, just like the cheerleaders in the eighties," says Pennington.

The nation's largest companies that train and outfit drill or dance teams is, of course, the National Cheerleaders Association and Cheerleader Supply. Though NCA's summer camps enroll 30,000 students, allure is intensified by the company's offerings of special events packages. The brainchild of Mike Miller, head of NCA's drill arena, event spectaculars range from participation in Ireland's St. Patrick's Day Parade in Dublin to Macy's Thanksgiving Day Parade in New York City, to participating in the parade and halftime shows at the Mobil Cotton Bowl in Dallas and the pregame and halftime extravaganzas for the Eagle Aloha Bowl in Honolulu.

Such extravaganzas provide students the opportunity to broaden their horizons as well as a chance to strut Texas stuff in foreign locales. For example, the Macy's parade package includes air and ground transportation, seven nights' accommodations, all meals, practice and performance outfits, which the students keep, a Broadway Show, a Radio City Music Hall show, and

Talking Heads David Byrne flipped when he saw the Apache Belles in their new black spandex outfits and immediately featured them in his film, *True Stories.* *(courtesy: Tyler Junior College)*

127

Thanksgiving dinner at Tavern on the Green. Not bad for roughly $1,300 a student.

Though the Rangerettes perform at various NCA-sanctioned events, Gussie Nell Davis has never liked NCA's merchandising. "Gussie Nell is not real fond of this company, Mr. Herkimer, or more particularly what I do for the company," says Mike Miller. "Basically she feels that we have plagiarized what she has conceived." His cheerleading sponsor at Kilgore College was Deana Bolton, the woman to whom Davis passed her baton in 1979, thus crowning her the reigning drill queen.

"Gussie Nell has created something that other people have expanded upon. What can I say? It's a free enterprise system," concludes Miller. Knowing firsthand the tenseness that prevails between cheer and drill factions, Miller could not have been more pleased when the 1989 Macy's Thanksgiving Day Parade was nearly cancelled due to a six-inch snowfall, bringing Manhattan to a standstill.

"It was much worse than it looked on television," says Herkimer. "The cold front dropped the snow at 2:30 in the morning and no one was able to make it into the city." With virtually no volunteers to carry the big parade balloons, such as Snoopy, Herkimer and Miller mobilized 350 of their cheerleaders and drill teamers in the middle of the night and taught them how to fly the balloons. "Those balloons would not have been in the parade without our kids," Miller says proudly. At 7 A.M., weary from no sleep and nearly frozen to death, the smiling high schoolers were ready. Ready to save the day.

"It was colder than hell and those kids worked their tails off and never, I mean *never* complained," stresses Herkimer. "The kids marched the entire route [and then] would turn the corner and come back to perform in

The contagion, a drill team staple, originated with the Kilgore Rangerettes. *(courtesy: Kilgore College)*

the routines they had flown to the Big Apple for in the first place. Sometimes the kids had to wait another hour in the freezing cold before they could perform. The chill factor was minus ten degrees. It was just like a tour of duty in Vietnam. You live through it and then you're so proud of yourself."

"The cheerleaders from Texas saved the parade," was the cheer from the parade commentators. Offered free rides by cabbies, the kids were showered with adulation wherever they journeyed for the remainder of their weekend stay. For the students, it was truly the experience of a lifetime.

But for others, such as Miller, the symbolism of such unquestioned cooperation between cheerleaders and drill team members, marching arm in arm, was a sight to behold. It was the call to arms that no student left unanswered. It was the smiles that warmed approaching frostbite. It was the distilled essence of true spirit leading. It was and *is* the spirit of Texas.

(courtesy: Tyler Junior College)

129

Oh, those Texas gals love drill teams.
(courtesy: Tyler Junior College)

(photo: Kent Barker)

CHAPTER 10

KICKING

An Afternoon with Gussie Nell Davis

UP A STORM

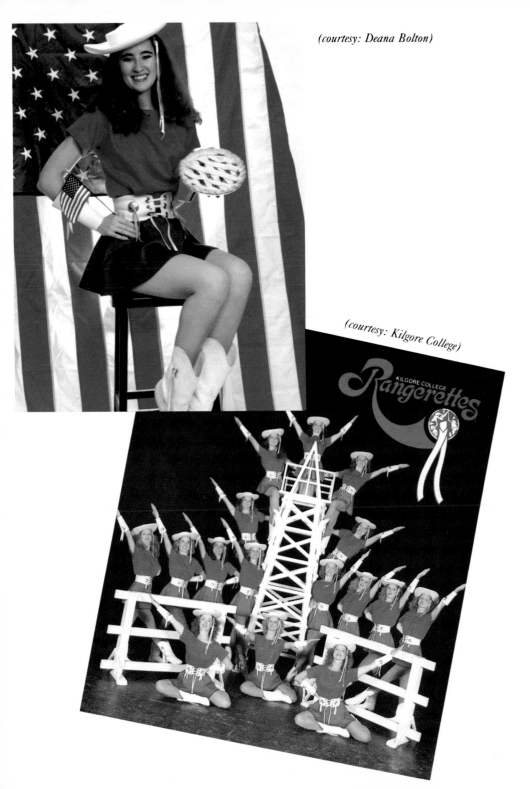

KILGORE COLLEGE
Rangerettes

Gussie Nell Davis, legendary founder of the Kilgore Rangerettes, lunches most days at the restaurant at Community Inn Motel out on U.S. Highway 259 in Kilgore. Occupying the same front table for numerous years, she scrutinizes the parade of townspeople drifting by the home-cooked temptations in the cafeteria line. In typical Texas grande dame fashion, she also perches where folks can see her.

On this particular cold winter day, her table was mysteriously empty. No one would dare dine at her appointed table. I had hoped to catch inconspicuous glances of Davis before our appointed hour. Fully aware that she easily could be recognized, she conveniently lunched elsewhere. Crafty woman, I thought. She's long become accustomed to big-city snoops like myself.

Opening the door to her medium-size ranch-style home was a neatly dressed woman in a red plaid faux Chanel suit, high heels, and perfectly coiffed hair. "I've seen you driving around town," she greeted me. "Everyone has."

Markedly spry, Gussie Nell possesses the contagious optimism of a high-kicking twenty-year-old trapped inside the body of someone less than half her age.

"Sit down and let's gossip first," she giggles. "I size people up the minute I see them. You're okay." After a few moments of raucousness, I turned on my recorder. "Just talk to me about your life," I told her.

"I'm not really that interesting, I've just worked hard all my life, that's about it." Apologizing for not having drip coffee, she admits to not possessing those huge coffee mugs like all of the men usually want. The dainty rose-painted teacups would be fine, I assured her. Setting a pot of instant java on the coffee table, she begins.

"I took piano all through high school and for four more years in college. [Drill] arrangements would never have been—drill team would never have been—had I not studied piano.

"When we started American Drill Team School in Dallas in 1953, there weren't any drill teams in the world except one or two junior colleges [Kilgore College and Tyler Junior College] and a few Texas high schools. And they didn't have directors. So all they would do is sit and let the kids do whatever, which was a disaster. So we started the American Drill Team School, the first in the world, so that the drill teams from the high schools could come there in the summer. We would teach them routines for the next year and then they could go back and have something that was done correctly."

Davis originated the drill team concept "in 1928—before your grandmother was born, dearie! I finished at Texas Women's University and headed to California and stayed with my sister for a year to work on my master's at USC [University of Southern California]. One day my sister came in just before school was out and said, 'I'm going on a trip around the world for a year, what are you going to do?'

"I went out and tried to get me a job teaching school, but they wouldn't hire me because I looked like I was just out of high school. Well, I got a telegram from my other sister, who was by then married to one of the doctors there in Greenville, saying I had been elected to teach physical education and pep squad in the [Greenville] high school.

"What in the hell is a pep squad, I thought.

"While I was in California, I went everywhere, to every football game—we only lived about four blocks from the Rose Bowl. They didn't have dance squads—they had car squads and bands. That's it. Maybe a few cheerleaders—all boys—but no one paid them any attention.

"I put my sister on the boat for her trip around the

Gussie Nell's hand-sewn variation of the poodle skirt: the Rangerette skirt. *(courtesy: Kilgore College)*

133

world and I boarded the train back home."

She was intrigued right from the start.

"What does a pep squad do, I asked them? 'Well,' some of the girls said, 'we thought we'd go out on the field and let a bunch of pigeons out of a box [to boost spirit].' I told them: 'Over my dead body!'

"What we're gonna do first is make letters, like the bands did, and put them on our costumes. We looked like Purina Chow chickens." Davis tilted her head back in laughter. "That's the only kind of sweat shirts [red and white checked ones] we had back in 1928. But we had white wool sweaters made the next year—with a G on them.

"After a while I couldn't stand that [she is known for her impatience], so I had cute little red jackets made and we had little white cotton ascots with an F on them. Our coach at the time was Henry Frankle. He won state championships and his personality was like lightning. If he was lightning, then we were the flashes that followed.

"So we became the Flaming Flashes. I couldn't stand it, though, because I wanted to dance on the field. They wouldn't let us. Greenville was a churchy town—people there drank like mad on Saturday night, sat in church on Sunday, and voted dry on Monday. So I started doing little steps with the band. Not quite like the colored bands in Mississippi or Alabama, but similar.

"One day we were working out on the football field [and] something reflected out of the corner of my eye. I walked over to this little guy from Baylor and asked, 'What in the world do you have in your hand?' 'It's a baton,' he said. 'What do you do with it?' I asked. 'Twirl it,' he said. See, up until then, wooden batons had a braided cord around them—the army still uses them. We'd never seen them. Well, I demanded he show me what you do with it. The basics were simple. So I got all the girls together to fork over ten dollars each, that's like eighty dollars now, to have this friend of mine who did woodworking make these wooden sticks and counterbalance them with a different size ball on each end, then paint 'em white.

"We *twirled* them," Gussie Nell proclaimed gleefully. "That's when we started to dance!"

"Then, before I could do too much of anything and get everything started, like getting approval from folks in the stands and not getting fired over the dancing, the band director had to teach me how to blow a bugle and how to beat a drum so we could play with the band.

"I was a stickler. *Every* march had to be perfect. *Every* step, *every* turn. *Everything.* I was just about as fussy about the tones that came out of those bugles. So then we came on the field with our drums and bugles, marched with the band and did a little formation, too. Next, we would perform [without the band] one or two pieces like 'Semper Fidelis,' that we could play ourselves. Then we'd *dance.* Finally, we'd put our drums and bugles down, pick up our batons, and go back and *twirl.* Dance twirl, I mean. It wasn't called that then. We were just twirling. We were doing all that when they called me to come down here [to Kilgore]. 'Cause the man wanted something at halftime that would keep people in their seats.

"It wasn't time to do the high kicks yet. Of course, it just broke my heart 'cause I wanted to cut loose." Davis does feel that the high kick was the fulfillment of her destiny. "But I did like to eat and have something to pay for my clothes and all.

"When I came down here [to Kilgore College] to see Dr. Masters, I asked him if he wanted a drum and bugle corps [similar to the Greenville High School unit Davis had worked so diligently to perfect], and he said *no!*

" 'Well, what do you want?' '*You* figure it out,' he told me."

The Rangerettes have only one rule: A Rangerette is always in class unless she is sick in bed, all the rest is tradition. *(courtesy: Kilgore College)*

Gussie Nell knew her time had come. Fate had dialed her number.

" 'I've wanted to dance all my life, that's all I've ever really wanted to do. I'm going to put a bunch of girls out on that field. If they do good dancing, it'll be *me*. If they make a mistake, it'll be *mine*. Not theirs.' [Dr. Masters] had a hard time getting the board to say yes. There had never been anything like that in the world. Finally, they agreed. But not 'til October [1939].

"People in Greenville couldn't believe it when I told them about being hired at Kilgore. They still treat me like a queen. I'm the only woman in their high school football Hall of Fame." Davis puffs up with pride.

One quickly surmises (and friends confirm) that Gussie Nell Davis accepts *all* accolades and dubious honors with an evenhandedness few ever master. Riding as grand marshall for the Longview Christmas Parade is just as thrilling for her as the president of the United States coming out of the crowd at the Cotton Bowl to shake her hand.

"I started out the rest of that year teaching the girls a lot of things like dance steps and formations. I also taught all the phys-ed classes, including one health class with all the football boys. Before the year's end, I called the girls in and said, 'I'm going to have this drill team, would you like to be a part of it?' "

Out of the four hundred who tried out, Davis chose thirty-three. Tentatively named the Petticorps, the original concept never materialized. Davis waves the thought away as unimportant. There are *no* sketches or photos of the original drill team look. The Rangerettes were her baby, the Petticorps were the bath water. The following year, Davis would expand the team to sixty-five girls, of which the best forty-eight would perform on any particular day while the others rested as alternates.

"I had to teach them everything. They didn't know

their right foot from their left. They didn't know how to turn their heads. They didn't know how to stand up and look like *somebody*. They didn't know how to dress when we went off to perform.

"We went somewhere that very first year—International Lions Convention in New Orleans. We didn't do very much the next two years. . . ."

"What about television?" I interrupted, something I forgot one never does to Gussie Nell Davis, and got a minilecture about how I didn't understand anything she had told me.

"Pay attention. I'm a pioneer. My name is Pioneer Gussie Nell Davis! Nobody has done what I've done. No one has been where we the Rangerettes have been and performed."

Regaining her composure, she pauses, seemingly relieved that I was not attempting to discredit the girls. She resumes conversational control in a manner that would cause assertiveness trainers to salivate.

"Even the outfit was so perfectly designed that nothing has been changed. Except the skirt. Started two inches above the knee. I was a devil for those short skirts. Nobody could have gotten away with that," she tells me, making a point with her index finger. "But I did."

"The Rangerettes' uniforms were designed so well that it hides that fact that we sometimes have a ten-inch height spread among the squad. Fooled you, huh? The illusion is a good one," she laughs hysterically. "Everyone thinks they are the same height, I love it!

"We don't have a weight limit, either," she continues. The girls, however, do weigh in weekly on an old-time upright scale shaped like a fat man with the word *liar* inscribed at the top. "As long as the girls don't look fat, why should I care what they weigh? A waste of time.

"Those outfits come in sixes, eights, tens, twelves,

High falutin' high kicks, the Kilgore Rangerettes in Cotton Bowl Parade. *(courtesy: Kilgore College)*

and a few fourteens. Blows everybody away. My illusion works pretty good, huh?

"We did fine until the war [World War II], and then . . . no football team. There was nowhere to perform, nowhere to go. That's when I went in to the president and said, 'I *can't* let the Rangerettes die. If they die, I'll never get them back again. In Greenville, we had a show to raise money, why couldn't we have one here? Let everybody in school participate so that everybody feels like they're doing something. Let's call it the Ranger Round Up.' So we decorated the old gymnasium and had fun.

"Bottom line, we kept the Rangerettes going. While everyone else was scrambling to get their squads together after the war, we were ready to take off for the Rose Bowl the minute the football teams came back in 1946. Been going ever since.

"Our way has been paid wherever, or we didn't go. The girls *never* paid for anything. Our shows in the spring [Ranger Revels] have paid for everything, every bit of material, everything except opera hose . . . they have to buy that. The girls were not out anything. We have it in our Rangerette bylaws that no girl can sell anything to raise money for the group. The board knew that when you start selling pencils, you're begging. The board didn't want any begging—*we're above it. Never* have, *never* will.

"Everyone's copied us or tried to say they were the first. But they were not, 'cause we were. They miss the point.

"The first and main reason for the Rangerettes is for the women to accomplish something for themselves. Without football, we wouldn't have had Rangerettes, of course. But it was always the team. The band. All boys. Nothing for the girls, back in those days. This gives the girls something to belong to where you teach them how to walk, how to stand, how to talk, how to sit, how to pick up things off the floor, how to walk up steps and down, teach them how to shake hands, how to be introduced to people, how to walk in and ask for a job and get up to leave gracefully. All of those things that help a girl morally."

One has to remember that until the late 1970s, Texans with privileged backgrounds sent their daughters to Neiman Marcus finishing schools to smooth out the rough edges. No such training existed outside that realm excluding exceptional parenting. Therefore, Gussie Nell Davis and the subsequent drill team phenomenon prepared girls of different socioeconomic backgrounds with needed confidence-building lessons in poise and self-assurance. This is something Davis is *extremely* aware of.

"I'm sure those girls did what all the girls today do, but I damn sure didn't know it. *Sex* is a word I have never used with my girls and never will. Sure I tell them that when they're out there on that field to forget that they're momma's little girl and *project*. After the game they can be momma's little girl again."

Herein lies part of her mystique: short skirts coupled with virginal innocence. She blasts her critics, denying any blatant sexual exploitation.

"If there's anything I can't stand—it's these old mennish women . . . that ERA bunch [from Houston, periodically charging Davis with perpetuating sex-object stereotypes]. . . . Listen, I think if a woman does the same job a man does, she ought to get the same salary. But just because she's a woman, that doesn't cut it. Not right. Besides, the ERA people are ugly. Don't even walk gracefully.

"God only knows how hard I've worked. I had to make all my props. You don't know the businesses in these United States that have started from what I started.

Gussie Nell created a truly unique living American art form: the all-girl precision dance/drill team. Then she took them on the road to share them with the world, and they loved them. *(courtesy: Kilgore College)*

"I was hard as nails on all my girls, just ask 'em," says Gussie Nell. "But I had to 'cause they had to be perfect. And they are." *(courtesy: Kilgore College)*

That sell props, plastic, pom pons, all the things you use in routines. We have the American Drill Directors Convention [in Dallas], mostly Texans. And you know, we have over one hundred booths. Our people selling stuff that is a direct offshoot of the Rangerettes. So see what I did?

"Everybody's jealous of us! I just laugh about it, 'cause they aren't as good as we are. Never will be. Can't be. They don't practice enough! You have to stretch every day, even on Sunday. I don't think the Lord considers it 'work.' It's simple. These kids have two things to do: go to school and Rangerettes."

Which brings us to the one-and-only rule Davis saddles on her girls: a Rangerette is always in class unless she is sick in bed. All of the rest is tradition. Critics and fans alike have marvelled over the Rangerettes' military-style code of address toward one another and their superiors.

"The way they [Rangerettes] say 'Yes, ma'am, thank you Miss Davis' or 'Yes, ma'am, thank you ma'am'?" she says smiling like a proud mother whose daughter has done well at recital. "I didn't teach them to say that. They pass it down from one group to the next. They want to do it. You know, it *thrills* me, though. Probably started as a reaction to my being so gall-darned tough on them," she speculates. "There's a lot they pass down, though. I couldn't even tell you how to lace up that belt."

Davis bristles at comparisons to the Dallas Cowboys Cheerleaders.

"If they could just once kick a straight line, I'd take back everything I've ever said about them," she laughs impishly. She knows what a mouthful that would be. "They don't practice enough."

"Did you know that nobody, nobody, not even Schwarzenegger likes to exercise. It hurts. It's physical. And nobody wants to take the time and they like to skip it. All right, if you think high kicking isn't hard, you come join the group and learn to stretch every day."

Critics have charged that her signature high kick is unnatural and physically harmful for some of the girls. "Hogwash," she says, raising her eyebrows. "Jealousy again."

One of her most thrilling moments came in the late 1940s, when she went to New York City to see the Rockettes for the first time. Even then she felt she had to check out her competition.

"My mouth flew wide open, and it stayed open until they got through performing. When they finished, I stood up and screamed, 'Great, wonderful!' I was so excited, I couldn't sit still. I looked around and I was the only one standing up and clapping. Everyone looked at me like I was some kind of idiot. They were used to them. To me it was the most gorgeous thing I had ever seen. I didn't know anybody could do it. They do the waist-high kick routines and it's pretty 'cause it's so fast. I came back inspired to do even more."

Hard work and singularity of purpose, not luck, is her prescription for success. Many are unaware of the dedication that history making demands of its loyal subjects. For some, like Gussie Nell Davis, the choice was between marriage and the Rangerettes.

"You *cannot*, and I don't care who says it, ole Helen Gurley Brown included—you *cannot* do two things this successfully—like have a husband and have a drill team. Drill team keeps you busy at night, afternoons, it keeps you tied in knots all the time. You have games Thursday, Friday, and Saturday. [The Rangerettes perform at all Kilgore College athletic functions in addition to their busy international bookings.] You're off on trips, you have to make money, you have to plan the shows. It keeps you on your toes all your time. OK, you got a husband over here. He'd like to see you

"You gotta love it . . . cause it shows in the eyes," Gussie Nell cautions Rangerettes. *(courtesy: Kilgore College)*

"I did it, didn't I?" In the fall of 1989 it was announced that Gussie Nell Davis would be inducted into the predominantly male Texas Hall of Fame. *(courtesy: Kilgore College)*

142

once in a while. He'd like you to come home . . . quietly.

"I'd been dating a lovely man the first year I had the Rangerettes." She looks away, and for the first time, vulnerability clouds her eyes. "I was going to get married the next year, then the next—that's what I kept on telling myself. One more year. Hoo, hoo . . . it [the Rangerettes] was getting too exciting." Soon she would have had to free herself of one at the expense of the other.

"I guess I made the decision to choose Rangerettes about 1950. It was either one or the other. No regrets, I've never looked back. I love what I've done. I've certainly had honors. [Governor Clements recently named her as one of 1990's Outstanding Women of Texas, something Davis is extremely proud of.] I've rubbed shoulders with every president since the war. Some have even stopped by my house to talk to me. Aren't you tired of me? I don't get to reminisce with anybody."

I found that hard to believe. Davis is a living legend who has stuck around long enough to see herself go down in the annals of history. She's also outlived most of her cronies. Maybe we Texans take her for granted in the same way New Yorkers did the Rockettes many years before.

"You see, girls like to belong to something. But not many girls can play tennis. Not many girls can play volleyball. Not a lot of girls can be cheerleaders. But a whole lot of girls can be in the drill team, understand?"

Recalling her most embarrassing moment in the last eighty-five years required little thought.

"Lordy, that's easy. I've told them [that] if you have to take nails and drive them into your head, I don't care. But that *hat* does not come off. Not on a football field.

When you lose your hat, everyone's eyes follow that hat to see where it's going.

"I've never concerned myself with how they stick them on their heads. They use bobby pin after bobby pin after bobby pin. Of course, you have that strap that's tied under their chin. In fact, it practically chokes them," she giggles.

"One of my most embarrassing moments was one time a hat flew off in heavy wind at the Cotton Bowl. As soon as the girl whose hat had flown exited the field, I chewed her out good. I never was so mad in my life! The parents came over and were real sugary, like, 'Now, Miss Davis, these little things do happen.' *Not* to Rangerettes they don't! It is not done because it absolutely wrecks the routine. I will *not* allow it. Well they couldn't understand why I didn't forgive her. 'She's your daughter, not mine. And I guess that's the only thing that really embarrassed me.'"

Contrary to what most may assume, stardom rarely follows the Rangerettes once they leave their uniform for the next crop of high kickers. Oh, there was Alice Slawn, Lawrence Welk's first Champagne Lady, but that's truly about it. Some say Gussie Nell Davis works all of the entertainment interest right out of their systems. Others claim that it's their founder's parting words of wisdom.

"When they leave Rangerettes, I tell them: 'Go on and do something, start making yourself knowledgeable of the world. Learn things. Forget this. This is just an incident in your life—a memorable one and you've had fun. Grow.' But I'll tell you one thing—they don't remember the routines. Oh, they might remember a step or two but they won't remember a whole routine. They *will* remember lessons in life I've taught them. If you don't believe me, I have thousands of letters to prove it."

Gussie Nell created a timeless look and signature pose that have weathered more than fifty years. *(courtesy: Kilgore College)*

Competition is fierce for those wanting to be a Rangerette. Gussie Nell has no patience for imperfection. *(courtesy: Kilgore College)*

(courtesy: Debbi Blocker)

CHAPTER 11
TEXAS
CHEERLEADERS
WHO'VE DONE GOOD

(courtesy: Tisa Weiss Hibbs)

(courtesy: J. Allen Hansley)

145

Liz Carpenter truly was baffled when I called her requesting permission to use her infamous hot tub as the photo site for the University of Texas cheerleaders.

"You gotta be kiddin' me," Liz barked. "Why, I'm not even a cheerleader. Besides, you know I don't let just anyone in that tub." That tub, which has been featured in *Time* and *Newsweek*, sits atop a massive cliff outside her patio in Westlake overlooking Austin, the Texas state capitol, and the University of Texas campus. Dignitaries from distant shores have soaked aching joints in the bubbles while sipping on another kind of bubbly, only to grow tense arguing the political and social dilemmas of the day.

Carpenter found the thought of Longhorn cheerleaders braving the 34-degree chill to splash in her hot tub mildly amusing, but she proudly waived consent. "But I do draw the line," she assured me, "right in front of John Connolly's toes. Yep, right there is where that invisible line is." Connolly, a former Texas governor and high school cheerleader from South Texas, and Carpenter are noted for their legendary banter, however good-natured and friendly.

"She was *not* a cheerleader," protested one of the girls on the cheer squad. "You know, Farrah. It was that incident in the Tri-Delt shower back in the sixties." No matter the level of Hollywood notoriety that Farrah Fawcett has attained over the years, some rumors just don't die. The crux of the matter is simply that Farrah was never a member of the collective society called Texas cheerleaders and the University of Texas squad wanted that fact made crystal clear.

Turning the tables on me, the cheerleaders questioned me as to whom I considered Texas's most famous former cheerleader. "No competition on this one," I conferred smugly. "Aaron Spelling." The response was perplexed

Kim Dawson model Tisa Weiss Hibbs. *(courtesy: Tisa Weiss Hibbs)*

Syndicated columnist Heloise. *(photo: Brian Small)*

Rosie Hall, sister of famed Jerry Hall (a.k.a. Mrs. Mick Jagger), was a Dallas Cowboys Cheerleader for one season. (Hair, makeup, and accessories by Elaine Dodson. *courtesy: Elaine Dodson.*)

silence and fixed stares. "Who's Aaron Spelling?" one asked timidly.

Liz Carpenter had plenty of homemade apple cider to warm the cheerleaders' spirits on this wintry day, but as soon as they left, we settled in the study with something that more suited our adult tastes.

"Years ago, I was in the Hamptons one summer with a group of Texans including Democratic compatriot Ann Richards. It was during the Carter administration, so we felt fairly safe on such Republican territory. There was an incredible heat wave that summer and we thought we were just going to die. Here Ann and I were sitting on the front porch of this magnificent home when a limo pulls in the driveway with uniformed men pulling Louis Vuitton luggage out of every door. Out steps Lynn Wyatt, perfectly dressed from head to toe in a navy blue and white sailor ensemble and hat.

"Confidently she breezed up the sidewalk looking like a million dollars in her hose, heels, and full makeup, in this heat. Ann and I were sick 'cause here we were looking like Sweaty Betties. I told Ann that we should see if we could keep her out in the heat long enough to make her sweat, then we wouldn't feel so bad." Carpenter laughed like a little kid with a mission. "She never broke a sweat!" exclaimed Liz. "I gained a new respect for her that very day."

"I have been accused of that," Wyatt muses. "Never sweating, that is. It's something I learned while cheering for the [Houston] San Jacinto High School Bears. Never let anyone see you sweat.

"My husband [Oscar Wyatt] says I was a cheerleader then and I haven't stopped yelling since," guffaws Wyatt in her distinctive full-throated Texas laugh.

"I've been cheering on Texas charities for the past twenty-five years," says another prominent Houstonian, Carolyn Farb. The former cheerleader is known as much for her tireless efforts to fill worthwhile charity coffers as she is for her opinions.

"You've either got it or you don't," confesses Farb. "You can't fake it. If you do, you'll never be a great cheerleader or charity fund-raiser. The two are both things that get better as time goes by, accepting the challenges. I am 100 percent compassionate about my fund-raising. A fund-raising function is like my baby. Sometimes at four A.M., when I'm on a roll and everything's clicking in, I wish the rest of the world was up so we could talk about it."

"Keep moving" is the cheerleader advice offered from syndicated columnist and San Antonio native Heloise. Following the 1977 death of her mother, who originated "Helpful Hints from Heloise" years before while living in Hawaii, the younger Heloise found that staying busy helped ease the emotional trauma of losing someone so close. Like mother, like daughter; the second Heloise stepped into her mother's shoes to continue the advice tradition.

"There are always those who are everybody's all-American. Twenty years later, after you've been crowned the Magnolia Queen, is it enough to live on the rest of your life? I don't think so. Keep moving," says Heloise.

As a member of the Alamo Heights High School Spurs her junior year, the spunky teenage Heloise found herself without drill team shoes her senior year—she didn't make the cut. "At first it was crushing, not making the team, but when I realized I did not have to get up at 5:30 in the morning to go to preschool practice, it was pretty nice. At the time, all I could think about was how much work was involved. But reminiscing now has made me realize how much fun it was.

"Drill team teaches you discipline, which is especially good for kids who have everything. You learn that you are an individual; however, my needs do not go ahead of the group. It's a valuable lesson.

The 1989–90 University of Texas cheerleaders splash in Liz Carpenter's infamous hottub. *(courtesy: John Hawkins)*

149

"Good Morning Houston" co-host Jan Glenn. *(courtesy: Jan Glenn)*

Kilgore Rangerettes Laverne Tittle *(left)* and Suzy Farrington *(right)* welcome Ronald Reagan to the 1957 Tyler Rose Festival. After Reagan was elected President in 1980, both women dug this photo out of their trunks, framed it and placed it on their mantels. *(courtesy: Kilgore College)*

150

"When men in other cities talk about Texas women, they imply that there is a certain Texas look. I don't know if that's big hair, a manner in which we dress, or the way we look. And when you think of Texas cheerleaders, you *always* think of Phyllis George Brown, all American, polished and pretty, but not wholesome. That's the Midwest. A little glamorous and impeccably dressed down to her nails and shoes. That's Phyllis and that's the Texas cheerleader look.

. "It goes back to the old Wild West–John Wayne type days when you had to have the guts to obtain the glory. Texas women literally took care of the ranch, gave birth, and went out the next day to do chores. It's what we do.

"As a cheerleader, people are always watching you. You can't roll out of bed Saturday morning and head to the coffee shop, because someone might see you not groomed. Whoa, bad news. It's a heck of a responsibility. But what it taught me is that I can look presentable in five minutes. I take the time to do it for myself—even when I'm alone. It makes me feel better," laughs Heloise.

Phyllis George Brown is probably the embodiment of every Texas cheerleader's dream: junior and senior high school cheerleader, North Texas State cheerleader, Miss Texas, Miss America, ABC sports commentator, television personality, governor's wife, author, and freezer queen: Chicken by George. She cohosted the 1991 Miss America Pageant with Gary Collins.

Other successful former Texas cheerleaders include Marshall's Susan Howard, who gained national fame starring on the long-running nighttime soap "Dallas," and Mesquite's Jerry Hall (a.k.a. Mrs. Mick Jagger), whose little sister Rosie was a member of the 1970s Dallas Cowboys Cheerleaders when they burst into national prominence. But none has risen to the heights attained by Phyllis George.

An heir apparent might be Christy Ficthner, a former cheerleader, Miss Texas, and Miss USA. Though still the favorite of the six Miss USAs cultivated by Messrs. Guy and Rex of El Paso, the Kim Dawson model has yet to get her break into film or television.

One former Texas Tech University cheerleader who got her lucky break into television right out of college is "Good Morning Houston's" cohost, Jan Glenn. Goldie Hawn was the rage on "Laugh-In," and because Glenn possessed the same blonde perkiness and dimples, she became one of the state's original kooky weather girls in Lubbock, Texas.

"It was all so silly," laughs Glenn, "people loved seeing just how stupid I could make the weather reports. I was still so bad after three years that I did not forecast the killer tornado that blasted Lubbock in the early seventies. I told everyone to go out and enjoy daylight

Kay Bailey Hutchison cheered the Longhorns to an undefeated national championship in 1963 while in UT Law School. *(courtesy: Kay Bailey Hutchison)*

151

Before starring in Hollywood movies and winning Oscars, Sissy Spacek was an active majorette in Quitman, Texas. *(courtesy: J. Allen Hansley)*

Former cheerleader and now Houston socialite, Lynn Wyatt as she appeared on the cover of *Town & Country* in June of 1985. *(courtesy: Norman Parkinson)*

savings time. Before I got back to my house, the storm came and blew half the town away. That was the last time I ever did the weather. I was history," she says, throwing up her hands.

College cheerleading for Jan Glenn meant trying to keep her [male] partner sober enough so as not to drop her at Southwest Conference football games. "We weren't nearly as serious about cheerleading in the late sixties as the kids are today," she confides. But one of her most important career lessons was learned on the gridiron sidelines, later enabling her to command the nation's number-one-rated local television program, "Good Morning Houston."

"Whenever you are in front of a crowd leading cheers, your movements have to be big; when you are in front of the camera, the same is true. Everything has to be bigger, it has to have more energy, more excitement, because TV is shrunk down to where you're only this big. You need a motion like this [she motions big with her hands]; it comes off small like this [she motions small] on TV. When people seem to have no energy on screen, it's because they don't understand how TV shrinks you and how much you have to punch it up. In that way the two are very similar."

Her best interviews were with country crooner George Strait and current heartthrob Patrick Swayze, both native Houstonians. Her most embarrassing moment, discounting animals (which under the hot lights always eliminate waste immediately), was a live interview with Cathy Lee Crosby in which a phone caller asked for the location of her G-spot.

"Whatever I do in life, I will always be a cheerleader," muses Glenn.

For young Dallas socialite Brooke Stollenwerck, overcoming embarrassment helped her make the Hockaday cheerleading squad. It seems that one day

152

young Brooke was running late to cheerleader tryouts. In front of the student bodies of Hockaday and St. Mark's (all-girls and all-boys private schools), she tumbled onto the gym floor, and the crowd roared with laughter. Not until later in her routine did she realize that she had forgotten to trade in her psychedelic tennis underpants for the required stretch pants. Oh, for the days when such things would still make us blush!

"I still don't know whether I got elected cheerleader for my vaulting or my underwear," says Stollenwerck. "I was mortified at the time, but it takes a lot to embarrass me now."

Stollenwerck has always been known to do things in a big way. Her 1976 Idlewild debutante ball, appropriately titled "Brooke's Bash," was held at the Dallas Convention Center. With a circus theme being kept as a secret until the last moment, partygoers actually walked into three rings of the Ringling Brothers, Barnum and Bailey Circus, complete with thousands of stuffed animals to be won along the midway. Proclaimed by author Cornelia Guest in her book *Debutante's Guide to Life* as the largest debutante ball in American history, Guest questioned, "How can a mere deb hope to compete?"

Dallas attorney and newly elected State Treasurer Kay Bailey Hutchison was the first female University of Texas law student to lead Longhorn cheers. "My professors would have to dismiss classes early so that I could trot off to the stadium," she laughs.

"In 1963, we played Roger Staubach and Navy in the Cotton Bowl to clinch the national championship." Though they met briefly at the game, the two did not meet again until 1982 at a Dallas·Chamber of Commerce meeting. Since then the two have become such great friends that Staubach headed Hutchison's 1990 bid for state treasurer. "Every time Roger introduces me out on

The fabulous Scholz sisters (*left to right:* Stephanie, Suzette, and Sheri) were all Dallas Cowboys Cheerleaders at one time, and are not only prominent citizens of Dallas but authors of the book, *Deep in the Heart of Texas.* (*courtesy: Bob Mader © 1987*)

153

Houston socialite Carolyn Farb and her cerebral palsy kids. *(courtesy: Greg Lorfing)*

the campaign trail, he begins with, 'Kay has a real skeleton in her closet,' and goes on to tell how Texas beat Navy in the Cotton Bowl."

The next year, Texas beat Alabama and Broadway Joe Namath in the Orange Bowl. Not until the Reagan years did Kay and Joe meet again at a White House dinner. "I walked over to Joe and told him I was one of the UT cheerleaders at the game, and he just went bananas. 'We were robbed,' he said. We've run into each other several times since, and there's always a lot of good-natured ribbing."

The most important lesson Hutchison learned while cheering at University of Texas came from famed Longhorn coach Darrel Royal. When asked by the press corps about his reaction to the controversies preceding their Cotton Bowl victory over Navy, thus grasping the national championship, he simply responded, "We're ready." "It's my life's motto," Hutchison states.

For Leah Kay Lyle, Miss Texas 1990, her fondest cheerleading memories are from high school: "I've been a cheerleader since I was in the sixth grade, and my best memories are there, instead of beauty pageants. Cheering is a team sport, pageantry is an individual sport. Cheering is done for others, pageants are for yourself alone.

"My best memories are from when I was in high school and I helped teach cheering to younger girls at a weekend camp/slumber party. It made me realize that responsibility comes with accepting the role of cheerleader. We set the example for others, particularly those younger, and it's a challenge not to be taken lightly. What we do in life never just affects us, it affects all those whose lives we come in contact with."

Growing up in Tyler, Texas, Tisa Weiss Hibbs started emulating cheerleaders at age six and officially started her cheerleading career in the third grade. "Enthusiasm is the most important aspect of being a cheerleader, not sheer physical beauty," says Hibbs. "A great cheerleader can elicit crowd response with her enthusiasm, regardless of whether they are winning or losing." This attitude has made her one of Kim Dawson's most sought-after Dallas models.

"I can create the same excitement on film. Everyone always asks me if I was a cheerleader, because I'm so enthusiastic about my work," she confides. "I work hard to stay in shape so that I can keep up with the demands of a rigorous shoot—not every beautiful model can do that. I can start at eight A.M. and shoot until two A.M. and be as fresh as when I walked in the door. It's a discipline, and I learned it all from cheerleading.

"Your attitude shows both in person and on camera. Enthusiasm that is genuine is contagious. When it's forced, it's a disaster. It must be an expression of the heart."

No one worked any harder at being a cheerleader than Pamela Graham did back in the mid-1960s. Graham was one of the original high school cheerleaders from Irving, Texas, who doubled as a Dallas Cowboys Cheerleader before they became halter-topped dancers in 1972. "We worked so hard, and no one yelled back," recalls Graham. They did not realize then that professional football fans rarely followed the cheerleaders' spirited advances. "It was such a downer for us. Everyone just sat and watched us. It taught me not to give up. Because of the strenuous athletic ability required, my heart rate is still excellent. It's great for motherhood," Graham says. "I learned how to budget my time so that I could get everything done in a day that needs to be."

Judy London is the only six-year veteran on the present Dallas Cowboys Cheerleaders squad. Proudly following in the footsteps of sisters VonCeil and Vanessa Baker, who clocked eight and nine years on the squad,

Man does not live by gymnastic prowess alone. National NCA "Best Cheerleader" John Houston is surrounded by his fellow pomsters from McCullough High School, The Woodlands, Texas. Not even Houston's girlfriend, also a squad member, minded being bested by the group's only male cheerleader. *(courtesy: National Cheerleaders Associate)*

Texas Monthly magazine recently designated Dallasite Harriet Rose as one of Texas' original Grande Dames. *(photo: Kent Barker)*

156

respectively, she says this will be her last year before entering law school.

"For me, the most rewarding thing about being a Dallas Cowboys Cheerleader is not what we do at halftime, it's in the service we perform for USO tours, nursing home visits, and children's home visits. The nursing home visits are particularly special, because we go out to talk to forgotten people as if we were their grandchildren. We talk to them, hold their hands, hug them, give them a kiss. We give them something few do, time."

Ironically, Judy London is known by more people in nursing homes than by students at Southern Methodist University, where she recently graduated. "Most of my friends don't even know I'm a Dallas Cowboys Cheerleader," she admits. Few make the transition from student to screen idol. "Many of the nursing home patients know our names, and I try to see as many as I can once a week. If we're going to make this world a better place, then we have to love our people. We must take steps to make a difference."

For those who have proudly led Texas spirit into the 1990s, making a difference is the battle cry. Most of them work hard, but they also realize that their position provides them a springboard for leadership as well as a platform from which to give spirit back to the community.

Most cheerleaders past and present are not celebrities. Most names will not be remembered as household words. Their pride lies in the fact that collectively they are Texas cheerleaders. The kids of yesterday are the adults of today. They are the hope for tomorrow. The future of the spirit of Texas rests in their hands—this is a given. There are miles to go before they sleep . . . until the spirit is the best it can be.

Phyllis George Brown greeted by Nancy Brinker at the 1991 Susan G. Komen Luncheon in Dallas. *(courtesy: J. Allen Hansley)*

"Dallas" series star Susan Howard attends a Dallas society gala with friend Paul Neinast. *(courtesy: J. Allen Hansley)*

157

EPILOGUE

Where there is magic, there is life.
Where there is life, there is spirit.
Where there is spirit, therein lies the soul.

(courtesy: J. Allen Hansley)